NAKED TRUTH
The Fall and Rise of Dona Speir

by Dona Speir with Chris Epting

Library of Congress Cataloging-in-Publication Data

Speir, Dona, The Naked Truth, Memoir, Addiction, Abuse

Summary: Dona Speir tells her compelling, triumphant story from sexually abused young model to Playboy centerfold, B-movie icon, alcoholic/addict, to clean-and-sober advocate who now helps others as a recovery counselor.

ISBN: 978-1-939282-42-2

Published by Miniver Press, LLC, McLean Virginia
Copyright 2019 Dona Speir

Dona Speir® is a registered trademark

First edition April 2019

I dedicate this book to my son Grayson.
He gave me the courage to step into the light the day he said,
"It's your job to tell your story, Mom. I'm proud of you."
Thank you son. I love you and I'm proud of you, too.
Mom

Table of Contents

The Care Unit

June 26, 1982. This is the day I was checked in to The Care Unit of Orange, a detox and drug rehab facility not too far from my home in Fountain Valley, California. I don't even know how I got there.

My last memory before that was being all balled up in the tiniest of positions, my knees and elbows squeezed up against my ribcage in a cramped closet at the ramshackle crash pad of a local drug dealer I knew. All 97 pounds of me, skeletal and sickly, sucking on a red-hot glass pipe. I had snorted cocaine for years but had started freebasing a few months earlier. It's what addicts do. When a drug stops working, when you start developing an immunity to the effect, you go for something stronger. So for me it was now all about crack cocaine.

In the closet, the sharp, acrid aroma of my burning acrylic fingernails made my eyes water. Or maybe I was crying. I don't know. My hands were charred with dozens of burn marks, nails burned down to the nubs. My tongue was raw and bleeding and was still painful from all the smoke in the last few weeks. I was disintegrating. My ears had that deep, ferocious ringing that always happened when I freebased. I remember the bright orange glow in the pipe that illuminated my emaciated body. Somewhere, off in the distance, the Clash song "Should I Stay or Should I Go" kept playing over and over, stuck on repeat, just as I was. I was nearing the end of a several-day bender that was something out of a horror show death spiral into a freebase-fueled madness. I couldn't even talk anymore. I had lost all ability to choose right from wrong. Addicts no longer have a choice.

I had overdosed on massive amounts of Quaaludes and other narcotics a bunch of times in my life already, but this was different. This felt like the bitter, brutal end of the line. I was ready to die in that squalid little closet.

Freebasing cocaine was still a fairly new thing. People knew about it because of Richard Pryor setting himself on fire. There was nothing else like smoking crack and it was the single most destructive thing I could've been doing.

The entire cooking up of the "devil dust" was a seductive, spellbinding ritual. Gathering around the stove with all the clamps and holders, getting it all ready, produced its own tension and anxiety. The foreplay of anticipating what the drug would be like while you were actually creating it was almost perversely sexual—a dance toward death, but a dance nevertheless. And I fucking loved it. I lived for it. I thought about the drug every second of every day. It owned me.

The smoke off the pipe enveloped me in the closet, forming an evil, suffocating haze, coupled with the fire from the small butane blowtorch that I kept furiously firing up. I'd created my own little raging private hell. The walls started tightening around me. Was this the end?

Chapter One
Early Pain

The world I was born into was chaotic, angry, and very dysfunctional. Well, the household was, anyway. It was a time when families kept their struggles behind closed doors and your lawn was always manicured. Appearances mattered. Outside was pristine and perfect, but inside, dysfunction was often the norm. By the time I arrived in the winter of 1964, my parents had a loud house full of teenagers and young adults. (I am the youngest of six children, all of them fucking lunatics. Good lunatics, but lunatics in their own way.) Tensions were always high, and resources were tight. It was the '60s. My father was overworked and undereducated. He had married my mom right out of the Marines at the age of 21. My mom barely had a high school diploma. Dad had been raised in what were essentially foster homes, with no real nurturing. He was trying to make ends meet, going to school at night and working all day. That was his life—he was tired and frustrated as he worked hard to put food on the table, but his solid work ethic soon gave way to acting out his anger: yelling, shouting, and my mother throwing things in return. All of this seemed normal to me when I was a little girl. My family had begun to enter some serious growing pains when I arrived. Timing is everything. It would soon level out, but my early years were rough.

Some of my earliest memories are not pretty, but rather loud and scary. I would run upstairs for the safety of my little room, pulling my drawers open and looking at my tiny clothes with animals on them. They were called GRRRAnimals, the kind that you matched by the animal prints. I would look at each little pair and say, "Don't worry, I won't die in you." That was me, making sure everything that was in my control was all right, wanting them to know that when I was buried, I would not make them go deep underground in the dark with me. Was this normal? Having feelings for everything like this? These kinds of thoughts at 6 years old? I don't know. But it was me. I was sensitive to a fault.

In that era, my father used a belt on us kids. It was his way of showing us right from wrong. And, in some bizarre way, that he cared about us and wanted us to know he loved us. My mom, on occasion, would use a wooden spoon or hairbrush, or anything she could grab at the moment.

They were frustrated and short-tempered and lashing out.

When my dad would strike me, it crushed me because I loved him so. I was born a "daddy's girl." I did not want those to be some of my first memories, but we get what we get.

The last time my father lashed out and struck me, I was in the 4th grade. Once again my brother and I were fighting about something trivial. Blankets or the TV or something. My father had yelled at us to stop fighting many times. We ignored him. But this time something within him really snapped. The next thing I knew, something struck my head. I ran to my room crying. My brother scrambled away as well. Back in my little room, tucked way deep underneath the covers, I sobbed.

I was in my new flannel nightgown with the tag that said "Made especially for Dona from Stacy." It was a white flannel nightgown with little purple violets on it. One of my girlfriends' moms had made it for my birthday. I had just received it and I loved it. It was the first time I had something so special with my name on it. My best girlfriend Stacy had picked out the fabric because my favorite color was purple.

I was crying so hard, everything was wet. My mother came in to check on me. She turned on the lights. The pillow felt soaked. I thought it was from my tears. The sounds of her screaming still resonate in my head. "Robert, she's bleeding... Oh my God, Robert... Robert, get in here..."

With my eyes adjusting to the light, I looked down at my sheets and there was blood everywhere. My little hands, my hair, my beautiful new nightgown. The flannel violets were red. I screamed, "What wrong with me? Mommy, I'm bleeding. Mommy, am I dying? I don't want to die."

"Get the car, Robert, now!" my mother yelled. "She needs to go to the hospital!"

My mother dragged me out of the bed and down the stairs. At the kitchen sink, she dumped water on me to see where I was bleeding from. It was my head and it was not stopping. My blonde hair was completely saturated in wet, crimson muck. I saw my reflection in the window over the kitchen sink, just barely, but enough to see my red hair. I screamed again, seeing what little reflection I could. This was a real-life nightmare, almost incomprehensible for a child to process. Real blood, real pain. Because of my father.

My father pulled the car out of the garage, I got in the back seat with my mom, and, for the first time in my life, I saw my father run a red light. I knew it was something terrible. My mother had blood-soaked kitchen towels on my head and blood everywhere on her. They were panicked.

This was new.

On the way to the hospital my mother and father talked to me. First, my father, speaking in a soft but solid voice. "Dona, you cannot tell them Daddy did this."

Then my mom. "Do you understand, Dona?"

My dad. "You will not be able to live with us anymore."

"Daddy will go to jail," my mother added.

"What do I say? I don't understand!" I sobbed uncontrollably. It was confusing and disorienting. I wanted to wake up from this nightmare.

Once in the emergency room, I received 17 stitches on my head after the doctors cut my new nightgown off of me. Why was I getting punished? Why my new nightgown? I loved it so much. I was devastated. I didn't understand, and everything was hurting me. The shots and the stitches. The strange noises on my head as they punctured me.

Then the moment they separated me from my parents. *Are they taking me away? Is this it?*

The man with the thick black-rimmed glasses started asking me questions. "What happened to you, young lady?"

I started to answer their questions and before I finished, I was stammering.

"Who did this to you? Did someone hit you? Did your parents do this?"

He was big, with a clipboard, and they took away my mom.

What had happened? I loved my daddy. I didn't want him to go to jail; I didn't want to be sent away. I didn't understand. I shouldn't have fought with my brother. In a big bed in the emergency room, the same man with the glasses hovered over me.

"I fell out of bed"

He stared at me, knowing I was lying. "Tell me how that happened to you."

"I hit my head on the nightstand," I said, rattling on and on the best I could, then calling for my mom. There was little they could do to break me. They were not about to start calling me a liar, not after what I had been through. Yet they were doing their job. They were doing the right thing. How many other little girls sat there and lied to them just like I had? Those were not easy jobs. He was not going to take me away from my family.

We rode home in silence that night, my torn and bloody nightgown balled up in a bag.

I was 9.

My father's anger changed from that day on. He would not strike me again. I think he was so stunned by the chaos and pain that his behavior caused that he snapped into a new reality, a reality where he could no longer hurt his little girl.

However, that was not the end of the pain that would be imposed on me by men. Hardly. In a strange way, it was the beginning of an even more brutal era for me.

Something I'd like you, the reader, to be aware of, is that those very early years were so loud and ugly that I had, for all intents and purposes, locked them away until I sat down to write this book. This was a truth that I was scared of confronting, because after all, who wants to confront the fact that their earliest years were ugly and violent? Who wants to think back and remember a tortured little girl, crying under the covers in fear of dying? Because of the man I loved and admired? The man who was my very hero until his last breath?

Dona Speir

Chapter Two
Growing Up

Finally, things settled. The anger quelled, and life calmed down at home. At least as calm as it can get with six kids. Thank God. Growing up in Fountain Valley, California, in Orange County, was about as traditional as it got in the mid-to-late '60s in Southern California. Our neighborhood was a pleasant sprawl where everybody seemed to know each other. Our house in particular became the focal point for a lot of neighborhood activities, from volleyball to basketball. I'm not sure why, except that we evolved to have a very inviting home and kids were comfortable at my house. My parents went back to being kind and inviting, what I imagined they were like before I arrived, and so our house was a good place to hang out.

My mom had an open door policy. Everybody was welcome. The fact that I was the youngest of six kids meant kids of every age were here. My girlfriends and I would bake on the big holidays like the Fourth of July and deliver our cookies and brownies throughout the neighborhood, where it seemed like everybody was barbecuing and the American flag was always on full display. It was comforting on many levels in the neighborhood. No one locked their door at night, and, on Saturdays, it seemed that everyone was washing their cars or mowing their lawns. You trusted everybody and knew the entire neighborhood's families by first names. It was like one big extended family from house to house to house. Always someone in the street playing kickball or their version of touch football. It just depended on what season it was.

On those summer nights when my friend Lori and I would lay back on the corner sidewalk waiting for that first star to appear, we would shut our eyes and make a wish. The sidewalk was warm and we would always whisper our wishes afterwards. We could just as well have been in Kansas. It was all so innocent. At least back then.

We also had a very traditional household. My parents, despite the earlier transgressions, deeply believed that families should spend time together, and we all wanted to. My mother was a stay-at-home mom and an excellent cook. My father worked for the same company for 30+ years until he retired. That was the norm in my neighborhood. There were many men who worked at the same company, including my other best friend Jill's dad. They all had the same routine. In the evening, all the men came home to the neighborhood around the same time. We would all be playing outside as the carpools emptied out, cheering excitedly at the sight of our daddies.

Every Friday night, my parents would have their friends over to play bridge. Like I said, very traditional and very '60s. We had dinner together every night. At 5:30 sharp my mother put dinner on the table. All that was missing was a clanging country dinner bell. My dad's carpool let out at 5:15 with the same three men for decades. During the warmer seasons, I was usually outside playing and waiting for him, running up and greeting him with a hug and smile. That was after I set the table. My mom sat at one end of the table and my dad sat on the other side. Dinner was always lively—fun with lots of laughter. For some reason it never failed that there was always an extra seat or two at the family table, filled by a neighborhood child or a teacher or, later on, by my sisters' never-ending parade of awkward boyfriends. Of course, the phone was taken off the hook during dinner so that nobody could interrupt our family time. That's how my dad liked it. To him, the telephone was nothing more than a potential family interruption. I was taught to set the table every night very properly and very neatly, placemats and folded napkins and proper silverware. I liked that. The routine and the formality was something I looked forward to.

We had one phone located in the middle of the house, downstairs in a hallway, so having private conversations was a physical impossibility. My older sisters always raced for the phone and argued with each other to get off. That was the typical teenage lifestyle I watched as three older sisters and two older brothers all stayed very active in their own worlds.

My oldest brother had left for the military when I was three. He was 15 years older than I was, and when he left, it seemed to make room for more kids to run around the house. My three older sisters were already young teenage girls by then. Their activities were endless: gymnastics, clubs of every kind, funny purple hair dryers attached to their heads, being homecoming queens, Miss Fountain Valleys, team car washes, comings and goings and comings and goings. But everyone was always at the dinner table. My other brother and my father fished together a lot during this time. Living close to the ocean as we did, they would catch ½ day boats off the coast and bring home their hauls. In the midst of all these girls running around there was always a large tuna or two (or three!) being cleaned in our backyard. My older brother, Jonathon, was always trying to get me to touch the eyeballs. Being the youngest, I was shuffled a bit, but I found my secret happy place. It was in the front yard in the ficus tree. I had swung and climbed the branches so many times that they had become smooth. I would hide out in the tree, and, when it was slightly overgrown, no one could see me. Though everyone knew where to find me, it was up high and it was all mine. My secret little nest.

Even in the middle of all this chaos there was order. And it was the happiest of places. Everyone wanted to be at the Speir's house because it was fun, open, and comfortable. There was always something going on from board games to barbecues.

Dona Speir

My father, despite what I have previously described, also had many strong and positive qualities. As a young girl, after waiting outside for when my father's carpool would drop him off at home, I'd be clapping and jumping alongside him as he walked in to see the rest of the family. I just adored him, even after what had happened to me as a younger girl. As far as I was concerned, I was an only child. That was my daddy and mine alone. Considering there were five ahead of me, that was strange, I know, but somehow it was easy to zone everyone else out. I just always had this deep affection for my father. Since I was the youngest and the age span was so great between myself and the oldest, he seemed to have more time for me. Nobody else was challenging him for attention, which is probably why I was so possessive of him.

Besides the fact I simply loved my daddy, just what was it about him that I locked onto? For starters, my dad was able to do everything. He could fix anything and he repaired everything in our home. He was a naturally skilled mechanical expert. He also had an amazing work ethic. I would join him on the weekends and he would teach me all he knew about everything. I was always all ears. My favorite place was at his workbench. To me, he had every tool imaginable and he taught me how to use them all. I learned how to make and pour cement. Lay bricks. How to strip and refinish furniture. How to prep and paint inside as well as outside. To this day I can patch drywall and cut and build any small wood anything. I was taught how to take care of my car, check my own oil, fill my own fluids, help change my own oil, and fix my own flat tires. For a girl, thanks to my dad, I was pretty handy. I knew more than most boys ever would.

But the best things I remember were the long and lazy Saturdays when I would sit with my dad and help him do his bills. I was a young girl who loved hearing his stories, advice, and wisdom. We would talk about all kinds of things, mostly about all that he had to learn on his own.

He had a tough life. His father pretty much abandoned him, and his mother couldn't care for him, so they left him with a foster family to raise him. The bill paying was tedious and methodical, but our deep and thoughtful conversations helped the hours melt away, and the time was always gone too soon.

My dad taught me about money. He told me never to spend beyond my means. To never have more than two credit cards. To always pay them off at the end of the month. To save my money and to put a large down payment on my cars and houses. He told me to never cheat on my taxes and to not mess with the IRS, the police, or the FBI. We always joked about the FBI. He was an honest man. A hardworking and loyal man. He might never have had much, but he had pride in everything he did.

Those precious Saturdays as I sat at our dining room table with his bill box, licking the stamps and writing the return address on the envelopes, were some of the best times he and I ever spent. That bill box always made me think of my dad. At that table I learned about life and I also learned about my dad. He was never very emotional or overtly expressive. He never said "I love you" to me. I knew he loved me, but he never said it. Much as I might have wanted to hear it, it was okay. I understood it just wasn't him.

Because of those lessons he taught me regarding hard work, I got a job starting in the seventh grade. I'll admit, it was a little hard missing things like afterschool dances and other social events while I worked my first job at the dry cleaner. I was making $3.50 per hour. I was given a small allowance at home and was expected to do many chores. Saturdays were for cleaning the house, not for cartoons and playing. Now I was working on Saturdays. I was learning the value of the dollar at an early age and I had no idea how important that would be as I got older.

The work at the dry cleaner was pretty easy. I would tag all of the dry cleaning and run back and forth to people's cars and do basically whatever needed to be done. I was a hard worker but the work didn't seem too challenging. I was a happy young girl and I liked to be with people.

Of course, I would often daydream about being back at home climbing my favorite ficus tree where I could get lost and get a sense of privacy that I never had inside the house. I cried on the day when the city came and cut my tree down along with a lot of other trees in the neighborhood. That was painful, but not as bad as something else that happened around that same time.

Me, swinging from my safe place,
my ficus tree, out in front of my house.

I wanted a new Schwinn beach cruiser bicycle and my dad told me that, since I was working, I could go choose one at the shop and pay it off in installments from the money I earned at the dry cleaner. That's the work ethic I was taught. I wanted something special. I went to the bike shop and saw the Schwinn of my dreams, a bright yellow beach cruiser with white wall tires and lots of stainless steel. It was a very special bicycle, a $140 beauty. My best friend Jill had the exact same bike, so, since we always liked to match wherever we went, this would be perfect. My father and I went to the new bike shop in town and I put a down payment on the bike. They allowed me to have it and make payments every week when I got paid.

But then I woke up one day to discover it had been stolen off the front porch of our house. I still owed a lot of money on that bike, and I continued working to pay it off. I was devastated, and it gave me a serious lesson about life. Sometimes you are on the hook, whether it's your fault or not.

I think my favorite nights growing up were Mondays because that's when *Little House on the Prairie* was on television. My special routine every Monday night was to take our little black and white television and bring it into the kitchen. I carefully balanced the little TV on a chair while I would bake cookies. For the entire hour I had the kitchen to myself. The older kids were out or doing homework and I was old enough to be trusted alone in the kitchen. The combination of my favorite show and baking remains one of my most magical memories as a child. Watching my favorite family and smelling chocolate chip cookies made from

14

scratch—nothing was better. The next day at school, my girlfriends and I would sit under a tree at recess and talk about the prior night's episode and what we thought—how cute Michael Landon was and how we wished he was our dad—and then, we'd all happily skip back to class, visions of "Pa" in our little heads.

Occasionally, one of my older sisters would take me to the Fountain Valley Drive-In movie theatre with her friends, which was always fun. But nothing compared to Monday nights in the kitchen.

Looking back on those days, it really was a special place to grow up. I worked hard and I played a lot and I was surrounded by good people. There was a lot of temptation awaiting just around the corner but that was a couple of years away. In the meantime, I was still free to dream about what I wanted to do when I grew up. And what was that? Well, I always knew I wanted to be a florist. From the very first time my favorite sister Paula took me to her friend's family flower shop.

It was the smell. It was also all women working there. They seemed so happy and I liked that. They were all stationed around a floral bench (much like our family's dinner table) working as a unit and separately creating beautiful things. They let me sit on one of their "adult" stools and clean long stem red roses, explaining to me how delicate they were and the proper ways to touch them. It was an immediate bond. That first day left an everlasting impression.

At home, we had the most beautiful gardens and yards, which added to my dreams of being a florist. My father did all the work. This was another talent of his: the ability to create and maintain beautiful grounds. From laying the brick patio in the back yard that my mother so desperately wanted, to building a lath house for her exotic ferns and fuchsias, he did it all. There's a reason our yard was the talk of the neighborhood. That was all thanks to my dad.

As a child, going to the nursery with my parents was an exceptional treat. It seemed my father knew how to take care of every kind of living plant. My mom also had a great deal of knowledge about flowers. Every fall, we bought bulbs, and, because we lived in Southern California, we would hide them in the refrigerator in paper bags until it was time to plant. They looked like dirt in these bags in the bottom of our refrigerator. I always had to explain to my friends what these were. But in the spring I was so proud of our gardens. My brother and I had our own vegetable gardens overseen by my mother, who planted artichokes, which were my favorite. We were always encouraged to spread our imagination. My sisters who were older would be in the backyard making sand candles and tie-dye clothing while I was planting with my mother and father.

I always loved that process of getting my hands dirty either by nurturing these beautiful things or building with my father. I think it was in my blood. It almost felt like a calling. Eventually, in the eighth grade, I got a job working at a flower shop and I never wanted to leave. I was hired by a florist who had an imagination like I had never seen. I was lucky to be in her shop. Every day I would ride my bike (yes I bought a new one) three miles to work. The Flower Cart was located directly across the street from a cemetery. People would come in to buy hand bouquets to lay on the graves of their beloved. To try and make people feel better, I would always put extra flowers in them with extra ribbon. It seemed to lighten their moods, even if just a bit. I could see it in their eyes. A little extra time and a little extra care. I knew then that seeing people hurt would hurt me, and if there was any little thing I could do to help them, I always would. It was there I truly realized why I loved the florist shops. It was a place where people came with their emotions. Men coming to make women happy. Or men coming to help fix what they did wrong. Either way, they would always want to talk about it. Share part of their story and open up about their emotions. Women on their wedding day, the biggest day of their life, and I secretly got to partake in the joy to make them happy. Celebrations galore: Mother's Day, Valentines, Christmas. There was always a reason to celebrate and to make someone's day better. To see joy in others, and, if even for a brief moment from the back of the shop and mostly without any notoriety, I could live and give, and it was filling my little 14-year-old soul with joy. It was just so natural for me.

I remember thinking: you learn so much about life and people working in a floral shop, if you just take the time.

Chapter Three
The Nightmare Begins

High school brought on all sorts of weird feelings for me.

I had gone from kindergarten through eighth grade with the same group of kids. It was about 40 to 60 of us. We were a tight bunch of kids and we did everything together. I was a smart student and was always placed in classes with kids above my grade. I was also placed in a Mentally Gifted Minors Program, but when I got to high school, it was different. We merged with so many other schools and my high school had close to 3,000 students. I was desperately lost and trying to find my footing. That feeling of being different and not fitting in really took over.

As if high school wasn't bad enough, during my first few weeks there, we had a break-in at our home. A strange young man in the surrounding neighborhood had a crush on me and actually broke into our home in the middle of the night. He crept into my bedroom. As I awoke, I screamed for my father, who came rushing in and found no one. The boy had slipped out. My parents took me upstairs and tried to calm me down, telling me I was just dreaming. I knew what I saw—I could even describe him right down to what he wore. As I went back to my room, I looked out the big picture window that was over our driveway, and there he was. He was staring straight at me from the middle of our driveway, as if he knew I was going to be there. I screamed again. My mom called the police and my father went after him. At least they finally believed me! I later had to identify him to the police, and when word spread around my school, it was more commotion than I needed. I had ratted somebody out. He had broken into my house, and yet I was the one who got funny looks of scorn.

Because of this incident, on the following day I missed my testing for my MGM classes that I was struggling to be a part of. This resulted in me not being in the class and thus I was now separated from my friends. I was now alone at this massive high school, feeling like an outsider and even an outcast. I needed new friends, and fast.

I'm not sure how I met Ashley, but she was like me, always happy and upbeat. She was super witty and held a job at a store called Miller's Outpost. I was at her house one day either borrowing or returning clothes. She had left me alone in her bedroom when her father, who I will refer to throughout as "Jack," appeared at the door. He had been a local fire department chief who had recently retired due to some kind of disability. He was very friendly and smiled a lot, like Ashley. His hobby? Photography. I remember Ashley telling me about that. There was something about the way he looked at me. It made me feel odd.

Stirring a mid-afternoon gin and tonic with his index finger, he said, "So Dona, Ashley tells me you're interested in modeling?"

I wasn't sure what to say. Modeling? I did not remember having that conversation with Ashley. Ever. He just continued. Now, I had never considered modeling. Jill, my best friend from grade school and I had taken silly courses from the local Park and Recreation department one summer when we were 9 but that was it. I had a lifelong dream of becoming a florist. That was my only career aspiration at that point. What was he talking about?

"Models these days are younger and younger, which is good for you," he leered.

I just looked at the ground, feeling uncomfortable. "I really haven't given it much thought," I said.

He called his daughter in. "Ashley, finish your makeup and I'll take Dona up to the studio to show her some of my work"

Ashley wore more makeup than most of the girls I knew, and she was older than me. I was always impressed at her ability to put on makeup. My sisters and I were all natural and I wasn't particularly good at those kinds of things. I was more rough and tumble, and a very good athlete.

Anyway, not feeling much choice in the matter, I followed him down the hall and passed Ashley's mom, sitting in her easy chair. Their home was much different from ours. It was darker, with the TV droning on all the time. There was something bleak about the scene. Ashley's mom was always sitting in her chair when I arrived. She was slightly overweight, with an outdated hairstyle, though always put together nicely.

She smiled and said, "Dona, would you like something to drink, dear?" She was friendly and I always felt welcomed by her.

"No thank you. I can only stay a few minutes." It was a Saturday and I was due back to help my father with chores around the house.

I continued up the stairs, and when I rounded the corner I entered a whole separate world. It was different from the rest of the house. It was bright, with light beaming through. It was very small but well appointed. Nothing out of place. Not like the rest of the house. There were a few black and white pictures of other women on the walls. They were older than I was. There were no cameras set up, but a crisp white paper backdrop rolled out in front of a couch. There were also a few lights with umbrellas and a funny smell. Jack saw me wrinkle my nose.

"Oh, don't mind the smell. Follow me." He led me into a small room that had trays with liquid and strings with clamps and negatives hanging from them. "It's only the chemicals from the dark room. It's where I develop my pictures."

It was a small, cramped space. Looking back, it was probably an unfinished bathroom or closet he had converted into a darkroom.

He continued the tour. He had a very small closet stuffed with clothing and costumes and a rolling rack of the newest bathing suits in the corner that would make any teenage girl lose her mind.

I followed him down the hall into a smaller room, and, like the others, it was perfectly appointed. Nothing out of place. It almost seemed like the entire studio wasn't part of the house. Sitting directly in front of a large makeup mirror was a director's chair. He directed me to sit down. He flipped on the light switch. The entire room seemed to glow with my little teenage face directly in the middle of the mirror.

The gray-haired man leaned down over my shoulder and spoke to me through the mirror. I could smell his Parliament cigarettes on his breath and see the slight yellow staining on his moustache. "This is where the magic happens. But you would have to learn all about this."

He uncovered the table below the mirror and it was every little girl's fantasy of makeup. All glistening back in the mirror at me. Large circles of color in all palettes. It was enticing and intimidating all at the same time. It was more than anything all three of my sisters combined had at one time.

I thought, *what in the world is Ashley doing downstairs when she could be up here?* I was still gazing at the mirror, noticing my tan skin in the reflection in between the rows of lights. Could I really be a model? He made this all seem so complicated, yet I just wanted to play with everything. But I got the impression that it was a "look but don't touch" scenario. Definitely don't touch.

As we walked out of the makeup room, he went on to explain that he had designed a "course" for beginners to start modeling and that I showed promise. I had never been exposed to any type of world like this before. He showed me sample works of his mentor, Peter Gowland, and explained how important he was in the photography industry. He talked as if he knew him.

He was eager for me to become one of "his modeling students." I had no idea at that point that this was a person who apparently had created an entire home-based modeling instructional course not so much to help girls model, but to help him molest those same girls.

He went to my parents and arranged for me to become one of his "students." They thought it was an agreeable idea, something I could do in addition to working at the florist shop, while going to school. Everyone always commented on how pretty I was, and I guess he made a compelling case to my parents that he could be the guy that could take me to the next level. The problem was, his levels were lot different than the very legitimate levels in the modeling industry.

No one in my family knew the difference.

I would go to the "studio" once a week, where, for the first part of the three-hour session, he would basically read to me about modeling and show me pictures from hardbound modeling books. He would teach me how to stand. He would teach me how to pose. He looked so ridiculous posing as he demonstrated. He would teach me how to look at the camera, using vowels as facial expression: *A-E-I-O-U.* After about an hour and a half of this, his wife would come in with a bit of lunch for us, usually a grilled cheese sandwich with a dill pickle on the side. We would eat and then get back to work, the second part of the session, where he would begin photographing me, with me practicing all the techniques I had just been taught. Toward the end of the session, his wife would return with a gin and tonic for him. I was to wear a leotard and he would pose me, touching my shoulders and arms. At first it seemed odd, him moving my limbs, but as time went on, it seemed natural. How else was I going to learn? The following weeks after each shoot, we would go over the pictures. With a big red felt pen, he would draw circles on every picture of everything I did wrong.

It seemed I did everything wrong. From my knees to my feet to my hands to my head. There were four pictures per contact page and every week every picture was marked with bright red circles and slash marks. I thought, *I must suck as a model.*

My parents would ask how it was going and I would show them my three-ring binder with my pictures all drawn up. Bright red. Every picture.

A picture that "Jack" took at "photo days."

For the first couple of months of this, it was fairly mundane. Eerily, we slowly seemed to be becoming friends. We laughed a little more and the red marker started to disappear on my pictures. Not on all of them, but more and more. I could see I was making him happy. We started talking about my personal life over lunch. He asked many questions and I told him about home and my parents and siblings. He asked all about my boyfriend, whom I had recently started dating, and told me about raising his daughters. He told me how he and Ashley talked about everything, including sex, and that it if I ever had any problems, I could come to him.

But I could always see something else brewing behind his measured calm and smile, which was always fueled with several gin and tonics after lunch. He would look at me far too long. He made me uncomfortable with the obsessive staring.

Then, things started to change. When I arrived at his studio we would start shooting immediately. He wanted to shoot me in different clothing. It was time to have fun because I had advanced, he said. He dressed me up like a little girl with pigtails and other provocative costumes. He would let me get into the makeup room now, always carefully explaining the makeup and contour. I always felt intimidated. It seems I never did it right. I never wore a lot of makeup and this was so complicated. Or so he said it was (to this day I still have insecurities about makeup application. Being told I was not doing something right for so long played a traumatic part in my wellbeing in many areas). Soon, he was always aggravated with me. I spent too much time doing something or I couldn't follow directions. He would come in and grab the brushes out of my hand, explaining to me over and over how I didn't do it right, how I couldn't contour or put on eye shadow, that it just didn't look right. But he did like the pictures. However, oddly, he wouldn't let me add them in my book.

One of the costumes "Jack" bought for me.
Little did I know he was grooming me.

On certain Saturdays, out near San Bernardino, about an hour away, he would often take me to what were called "Model Days." These were basically sad events where other photographer/model coaches would bring out their prettiest girls to show off and drum up new business. Driving out there in his RV was always a creepy experience. He would pack up his costumes and makeup. I would run out in these outfits and see how many photographers would gather around me. Then when the crowd would die down or go to another girl, I would change clothes, usually into something skimpier each time, saving bikinis to the very end. I could see him in the back of the pack of photographers, chatting and smiling, as if he had the golden goose: the prize. But he still had not laid a hand on me. That would not happen until we were about six months into his "training."

It started simply, in costumes, some cute, then more revealing. That was the pattern. He always had something new for me. Something he was excited to shoot. He would go out and buy new bathing suits that I could not afford and let me shoot in them. Or occasionally let me borrow them to wear to the beach. He bought me special clothes and accessories. Things I had seen in magazines or that Ashley had mentioned. He never let his daughter use them. Only for me. I was beginning to feel special. It was a very strange. Then one day, he asked me to take my top off and turn around. That it would be a better shot. I was in a bikini already, but to cover my breasts with my arm. For some strange reason, it seemed natural. My body was no longer something to hide; it had become something to shoot. Something to work with, as if it was a separate entity. It was no longer my body but *our* body to work with.

I don't know what happened first, his touching or the nude photos. But there it was. Him justifying touching me by saying, "You never have to touch me, Dona." Did he know the damage he would do to me for years to come? Did he even care?

I thought about telling my parents. But Jack knew, because we talked so much, that I had become sexually active with my boyfriend. So I reconsidered, thinking that by going to my parents about this photographer, this photographer might then tell them about my boyfriend. Like blackmail. I thought, *I just know this was all my fault and that I am a bad girl.* And I now felt trapped.

Dona Speir

My high school boyfriend was my first love. The very first person I had ever said "I love you" to. I risked losing him and he would find out about the naked pictures Jack had taken. I would be disgraced. Humiliated. Why, why did I take the pictures? Why did I let him touch me? How could I have done all this? I was blaming myself, even though in hindsight I see it was not my fault.

Jack became such a dominant character in my life. He had asked me so many personal questions and he knew so much about my boyfriend and me. Now I didn't dare push away for fear of what he might do to me. My parents would be so mad at me. This all played out for months. It became my dirty little secret. He told me the photos were more like "works of art" and that there was nothing distasteful or embarrassing about it. He promised me he would keep those private and away from the eyes of everyone, especially my parents. He started showing me other nudes of women he was taking. All of them extremely risqué in all sorts of terrible positions. I felt relieved because mine were nothing like that. They were older woman in lingerie but I had no idea he was shooting other woman naked. It was getting worse and he was wanting more and more, demanding more nudes, wanting more and more of me. Looking back now, I realize that this is something many predators do. That is, normalize the behavior by showing other samples of it. All of a sudden, it wasn't just me posing nude. It was all of these other women. So somehow that made all of what we were doing okay. Right?

Then came more "Model Days" in San Bernardino. After the event, he would now stop in the RV at McDonalds. I wanted to eat in the restaurant. Of course, he wanted to eat in the RV. I knew what that meant. There wasn't any escaping for me. After eating he would come at me and kiss me. We would end up in the back of the RV. I was stuck. There was no escaping this. It was only getting worse. The studio was bad enough but now this.

I would be there in the flower shop, cleaning up before we closed for the night, just dreading that I was due over to his house. In my head, I knew the lessons he had arranged through my parents would soon be coming to an end. Maybe this nightmare would soon be over, too. But then one night I got home from work and there he was, in the kitchen talking to my parents. I saw him through the window.

"She's doing great," he was telling them. "But I really think she needs to continue. She has so much potential, but I need to keep

24

working with her. She's making so much progress but we need more time."

Oh God. He wasn't letting me go.

I interjected. "No, you guys, I think I'm fine. Really. Mom, Dad, I don't need any more lessons. I don't want to model anymore"

It became a sickening blur. Jack telling my father he was behind in payments and seeing my father giving him a check. Explaining they had invested so much money and time. Smiling at them. Winning them over even more. I was sick. Physically and emotionally. My world was spinning, and it was out of control. He was there at my parents' home, *in my kitchen*. Was he going to show them the pictures? Was he going to expose me and tell them how bad I was? Was he going to tell them about my boyfriend and me?

By now my mom and dad really liked Jack. What wasn't to like? He had an impeccable reputation in the community. He was friendly and charming. He was my girlfriend's father. He was a former fire chief. Ashley had also been to my house numerous times. Everything was so normal on the outside. I wanted to scream, but I couldn't. I didn't want to leave the kitchen, but the heaving feeling in my gut was starting, and Jack had his hand on my shoulder as I ran to the bathroom to throw up. He was still smiling and chatting as I ran out. I know it seems like it would have been easy to tell my parents this, but we didn't have that kind of relationship. We just didn't. Plus, as I've said, I was also scared of what else might come out.

I continued going to his studio. My parents would drop me off, as I wasn't old enough yet to have a driver's license. As this all continued, I was becoming more than just depressed. I was becoming suicidal.

Dona Speir

The only picture ever published that "Jack" took of me.
A magazine to promote "model days."

Chapter Four
Helpless and Hopeless

The abuse I was suffering at the hands of Jack led the rest of my life to start unraveling. It was destroying me—eating at the fabric of my soul. As the months wore on, my grades suffered, and my home life suffered. I started drinking and taking drugs to help hide the pain. There is no way to overestimate the residual effects of a predator's abuse on a young mind. I self-medicated to try and make it all go away, but it just made things get worse.

My mind was always racing, and I could not get a grip on reality. I could not in any form whatsoever talk to anyone. I was drinking whatever I could get my hands on. I was smoking lots of pot and experimenting with other drugs. It got bad fast. Thanks to my out-of-control behavior, I had lost my best girlfriend Jill. I was seeking out lower companionship. Drugs were my only answer in my private chamber of hell. It was at this time, in my mid-teens, that I made several suicide attempts and overdosed numerous times. I tried hanging myself in my bedroom, and I was cutting myself on a regular basis. I overdosed on Quaaludes, and then after that Ludes, then just about anything I could get. What had started out as drinking as a teenager had blown up into raging addictions.

During this time, I noticed my parents fighting more, and they were sleeping in separate bedrooms. My father explained to me that my mom was going through the "change of life" as he called it and that things could be difficult for a while. I had no idea what that really meant. I had begun to smoke weed every single day by now and was drinking whenever I could. I was the only child left in the house and my mother and I were having terrible fights. There was no way I could tell her about the photographer. I had drifted away from the love of my father. In fact, we had all drifted apart slowly. The suicide attempts and the overdoses all blur together into one sickening cycle of abuse and self harm, and they landed me in the beginning of what would be many visits to a juvenile psychiatric hospital. People in the neighborhood began to notice I would disappear. Ten days here, six days there. Once, I tried to hang myself, but failed miserably. For weeks I had to wear turtlenecks to school to cover up the marks. But nobody close to us knew the real reasons. I would always lie and tell people I was modeling. I was the only person I knew who had ever gone to a psychiatric unit.

My first night in the first facility, after a botched suicide attempt I had made, was the scariest. I was brought in by my mom in the middle of the night. The floor was shiny, with the reflection of the blinking florescent lighting coming from above: bright, harsh, and unforgiving. You could hear people in locked solitary cells screaming from down the halls, moaning and wailing long into the night, as if in their death throes. Maybe they were. When my mother left, I was escorted to a room with four single hospital beds in it. No carpeting. There was another girl sleeping in the room. I curled up in the bed. It was cold and sterile. There weren't enough covers on me and the blankets did not tuck in. I was awoken by the girl sitting on the edge of my bed. She was talking to me, her feet dangling over the edge of my bed. I could see her silhouette through the florescent light coming in through the door. She was a having a full conversation without me and she was making no sense. I knew I was in the wrong place. I screamed, and a woman came running in. The young girl looked so scary with her long brown curly hair and deep, sunken eyes. She continued to talk as they walked her out. Wherever I was, I knew I wanted out. I remained on the high-risk locked-down unit for days. Eventually they allowed me in an opened unit that was still locked down, but the people weren't as crazy. Okay so a few had huge holes in the sides of their heads waiting for plates, but nothing as bad as the first few nights. I still refused to tell anyone what was going on. Tightlipped. I believed everything was my fault. What I know now is: I didn't have a voice. I had no way to communicate the pain I was experiencing. I was disillusioned. When they decided to release me, I could tell my father was ashamed and bewildered. He could not look me in the eye. He had no playbook for dealing with this.

As many times as I danced with death, nothing was as bad as the last suicide attempt. Because of my erratic behavior, my unstable home life and my excessive drug use, my first boyfriend broke up with me. For good. We had been on and off for months and it was ugly. Constantly fighting and drinking and fighting.

"Dona, What the hell is wrong with you? I just can't do this anymore, I'm sorry."

My world was crashing; I now had no one. "Don't leave me!" I screamed as he dumped me off on the beautiful lawn my father so handsomely manicured himself. "Please, I'll change, I promise."

"I'm done. It's over."

I sat there watching his little brown car as it drove away for the last time, turning the corner away from Walnut Street. I was heartbroken and crushed. Weeping, all the while saying to myself, "What is wrong with me, what the fuck is wrong with me, why can't I do anything right? I hate me, I hate me."

My inner voice was shouting, *see, you can't do anything right, you're defective, no one wants you.* At that point I was making an oath to myself, silent but strong, vowing I would never love another human being again. Never say those words. No love, not now, not ever. After sobbing on the lawn, I finally walked in the house.

My mother was yelling at me, "Where were you? You missed going to Jack's house. He's been calling."

I just couldn't face life anymore. I blocked out her screaming and walked into my bedroom and slammed the door.

My mom busted in. "Don't you slam this door on me, young lady… God Damn it, Dona!"

The screaming continued but I didn't care. I was internally scarred, and numb to the point of not even responding. The feeling of hopelessness and helplessness had taken over. I was completely defeated—alone and full of despair. My mother's voice only getting angrier as she slammed my door behind her. My behavior had hardened my parents. I was ruining everything for everybody.

There was an unusually large bottle of Tylenol with Codeine in my parents' bathroom. It had been prescribed to me because they had thought I had pneumonia, catching it in the florist shop from the chilly conditions. It was amazing I had never taken them. But this was the moment.

I proceeded to swallow every pill in the bottle, more than 50 of them. I returned to my bedroom and sat down in a large swinging wicker chair that my father had installed on a beam for my birthday three years prior. It was from the same eyehook in the ceiling that I had tried hanging myself from, when the cord I used broke. As I sat in the chair slowly turning, I began to fade. I prepared to die once and for all.

My mother kept coming in and out, yelling more each time. "Look at you! Now what are you on? Jesus Christ, that's just great, Dona!"

Each time she left, she slammed the door behind her. I ignored her. This is how I would leave the world. Being screamed at and berated by my mother. I was simply turning slowly in my chair as the sun was starting to set. The window was open and a soft breeze was blowing the little prism crystals I had collected and hung in my bedroom window. They began making beautiful colors in my room. Numb and fading. My gaze became weaker. As I was beginning to black out, my girlfriend Lori came up to my window. My friends always came to my window. It faced the street and it was their way of visiting. Especially if we were up to no good.

She looked at me and knew it was bad. I don't know what happened next, whether she called the ambulance or she got my mom, but the next thing I remember was the paramedic breaking into my room. I was lying on my bed atop my white satin comforter. They were trying to get an IV into my arm and they kept missing and spraying blood everywhere. Crimson splatter all over my white satin, my body, in my hair, and covering my legs. Mini fountains of blood. I couldn't talk, I could barely respond. I knew my room was crowded but I don't know who all was there, though I sensed many boxes of paramedic tools.

Deadweight and almost dead, I was loaded into the ambulance and, sadly, the neighborhood kids on bicycles were surrounding the chaotic scene of my house. Lord only knows how many I scared with events like these.

Once in the back of the vehicle, they raised my upper body so I could sit up and see above all the kids. In my foggy, drugged state, I saw my dad's carpool unloading. He got out and walked past everyone without looking up, briefcase in hand, head down. Nothing new here to see. That's how cold and hard things had become. Lord, what I was doing to people.

Soon after, lying in the emergency room, I heard a young woman on my left repeating urgently, "I can't get a pulse; I can't get a pulse."

I could feel my heartbeat in my throat; I didn't understand. It was weird. All these people with their mouths moving, no sound, hustling bright lights.

And then everything went black.

I awoke several days later, in intensive care, and I was more scared than I had ever been in my entire life. I felt extremely small in the hospital bed. There was no one around and the place was quiet and very dark. I was hooked up to monitors and I was alone. Incredibly separate from the world. No strength to fight. Probably more alone than I had ever been in my life. So severely frightened. Such a little girl. Physically and emotionally tiny. This was the first time I wasn't strong. I needed someone. I needed my parents. More than any time in my life. I knew it was really bad.

I started shaking and sobbing. It was as if I was 5 all over again and there was no one in the entire world. The nurses finally came around and told me I had been there for days, and that they were watching me for liver failure from the overdose and that my father was coming in soon.

When he arrived, he was in his business suit. He must have come from work and it must have been nighttime. He came to my bedside, but he was very cold and methodical. I knew he could no longer deal with these sorts of things. He stood by the side of my bed in this empty ICU ward for children.

I cleared my throat, barely able to talk, my throat sore from whatever they had jammed down it. "Where's mom?" I asked.

"She did not want to see you," he said, emotionless. "I just came in to sign some papers, Dona."

I started to cry. I had no idea what was going on. I lay there silent, looking for any sign. Anything. Any resemblance to anything familiar, any feeling. Anything. I was terrified.

With every little bit of courage I had, every bit of strength I had, every ounce of anything I could pull out of myself, I said to my father, "I love you."

Without even looking at me, my father silently walked away, never looking back, in the dark ICU.

Dona Speir

He had come to sign me over to a psychiatric hospital. Still covered in dried blood, I was admitted to psych, and my heart closed for good. From now I would feel nothing. I had nothing. I was nothing.

Chapter Five
High Risk Lockdown

The psychiatric hospital routine had become old news for me. On my earlier visits, I had really needed to be there. I was tired. I needed a place to dry out. Somewhere to go and detox for a week or too. I had begun to like them. It was easy. Like prison. To be told where to go, when to eat, sit, and talk, when to sleep and paint ceramics. I was tired.

This trip was different. It took longer to get out of the high risk lockdown. They had a hard watch on me. The suicide attempt was taken very seriously, plus my physical condition was poor. By the time I was released out to the open unit I was ready to run. I waited a few days and made a plan. I gambled money out of the other patients, playing cards, and also sold my medication. I called a friend of mine to back his car into the ally next to the hospital and asked one night if I could do my laundry. After hourly head count, I stuffed everything I had into a pillowcase including my duffle bag. I snuck out, climbed the wall, and threw everything over.

I was off before anyone knew the difference. He picked me up and dropped me off at someone's house who I didn't even really know. I met my lower companions there. The feeling of hopelessness and desperation filling every ounce of my soul. Empty and void, I sat on the curb and drank beer after beer. Then, after a few days, I went home. Much to the frustration of my parents. I think they now knew I could not and would not be contained.

My life was exceptionally dark. The men I had loved had turned on me. Hurt me deeply as I had hurt them. It wasn't until years after I stopped drinking that I was able to look at my part of the relationships

Dona Speir

to see how deeply I had hurt my father. I knew I had disappointed him time after time, but it wasn't until years later that I fully understood it. And it all started by being groomed and then sexually abused by a predator: Jack, the photographer.

One afternoon, after I had been home for a while and was back to "normal," I decided I wasn't going back to his home. I couldn't. I had begun to lose it emotionally. I was becoming severely mentally unstable. He was aware of my suicide attempts and overdoses, but always insisted I continue with "lessons" once the dust settled. But I was done with this shit. I knew it would cause big problems, me not showing up. My mom was not home, and I was supposed to ride my bike over. I just refused. I wasn't going. The phone in the kitchen began to ring. I needed something to keep my mind busy. I took an old pot and filled it with hot soapy water. I started with the baseboards in the front hall, scrubbing as hard as I could with a brush, like a maniac. The phone started to ring again. I scrubbed, still on my hands and knees, trying to block out the sounds of the phone. I put on the Michael Jackson "Off the Wall" album. It had just come out. With a new batch of water and a sponge now, I started on the wallpaper. The phone was still blaring. I turned up the music. I got a ladder to start scrubbing the ceilings. I was losing it. The room felt like it was spinning. The phone ringing and ringing. I was now on a different wall in the entry hall. The green and white wallpaper, water all over the floor. Moving hall trees and furniture, scrubbing as hard as I could, music blaring, in a panic, moving fast, when the doorbell rang. It was Jack. He was mad I had blown off the session and ignored the calls. I felt powerless. I obeyed. I left everything—ladders, sponges, pans, water—everywhere, in the entryway, and got into his car.

By this time, Jack was getting into hypnosis. He was studying a book and using these techniques to get me to relax. I was a wreck all of the time and he knew I didn't want to be at his home. Because I didn't want to be there, I went along with it. It was easier to pretend to be asleep than to be there.

Pretending to be hypnotized, I listened to him say, "I love you, Dona. I love you. And you will love me."

The feel of his mustache on my face repulsed me and I began to throw up. He had his way with me once more and then I got to go home.

34

My parents had no idea what was going on with me and by now I was becoming overly sexualized. My dressing was becoming different and I was screaming for help. I had become violent at home, putting holes in walls and slamming doors off the hinges.

My grades tanked. I stopped going to school. I went from an A–B student to hiding my report cards that came in the mail. I didn't show up to my job at the florist; I lost that job as well. My one favorite safe place. My mother drove me over and I had to go inside and tell them I was sorry for not showing up and they fired me. I got in the car and cried.

Though I remained careful to keep my mouth shut about Jack. Because I believed I was at fault.

I don't believe this is what caused my drug addiction or alcoholism; I believe I was born predisposed. I do believe however that this situation accelerated it more rapidly. What started out as smoking weed and drinking on the weekends with my high school friends turned into self-medicating with every kind of hardcore drug I could get my hands on. Uppers, downers, acid, Quaaludes, mushrooms, and any other kind of drug. That became my escape from reality. The fire chief had become my personal arsonist.

Dona Speir

Chapter Six
A Hidden Angel

Like some unplanned act of God, I heard about an agent in Newport Beach and I asked my mom if we could go visit her. I don't even know why. This woman, Marion Berzon, would turn out to be my angel.

As soon as we got there, she looked at the pictures Jack had taken of me and told me they were useless, each and every one of them. Not professional at all. "Garbage," she said with disgust. "Bad lighting, cheesy costumes—this is all garbage."

I think that caught my mother's attention. What had we been spending all of the money on, after all? And then Marion told us about an audition up in Los Angeles that was happening right then. As in that afternoon. We lived about 50 miles away from LA. It seemed pretty far-fetched. She kept insisting that we go and that I stood a really good chance of landing that commercial. My mom hated driving the freeways and I had my learner's permit by then so I told her I would drive. It was already mid-afternoon and we knew the traffic would be horrible. But we still had a chance to make it there between 3:00 and 5:00 p.m., the designated call time for auditions.

I had never auditioned for anything in my life. Yet somehow, I was hired on the spot. It was a Seiko watch commercial with Tatum O'Neil, which would be shooting for five days at UCLA. I had booked my first real modeling job that would pay me real money. But I had a secret nobody else knew. I knew that this commercial would allow me to stop having to go to that house on Hemlock Circle where Jack lived. This job

Dona Speir

was validation that I had what it took to get out of that house and never be around him again. Never. Ever. Again.

The Tatum O'Neil Seiko Watch Commercial
that rescued me from being sexually abused.
The beginning of my professional modeling career.

One problem solved. Though by now I had created many, many more. My drug and alcohol use had increased. I had destroyed my reputation. I had no friends. I had all but dropped out of school and my parents had no clue what to do with me. They were older, and they were tired, and wiped out from my horrific behavior.

They had tried every counselor and every therapist. I refused to tell anyone the truth. I was filled with shame. Everything was still my fault in my eyes. If only I hadn't let him touch me. If I hadn't taken those pictures. My suicide attempts had come to a stop, but I was severely depressed. I had stopped overdosing which meant no more visits to psych hospitals.

I was barely 16 when Marion Berzon sent me to my first real photographer for headshots. I was embarrassed because I sat on the stool facing the wrong way. I did everything wrong, yet the photos still turned out amazingly beautiful and that seemed to be what I might have a future in. Modeling. I had no real passion for it, but it found me, and I was willing to take the ride.

I didn't know the term "grooming" back then, but looking back on it, I know that's exactly what had happened to me. I had been a 15-year-old girl who had her first boyfriend, my first true love, and I wanted to explore intimate experiences with him. But the photographer had so warped my sexuality that I didn't understand what was right and what was wrong. He was the adult. I was a child. The problem (amongst

38

many) with sexual abuse is that it produces shame and guilt. Guilt for the action and pleasure received by the perpetrator. Shame that there was something fundamentally wrong with my own existence. I was now bad, damaged, irreparable. Worthless and of no value to anyone or myself. These are beliefs I would take into my adult life. I would have big red marks on me for years to come, just like those first photos, the innocent ones.

That said, little did I know how much worse things could really get.

Dona Speir

Chapter Seven
Opportunity Knocks?

Playing with Bill Cosby.

I often wonder how different my life would've been had a friend of my sister not been playing tennis with Bill Cosby in Las Vegas. She offered to take along my headshot, saying, "Let me show Bill. You never know what could happen." And she was right. You never know.

A day or so after he saw my picture, the phone rang and there was the one and only Bill Cosby, on the phone. He asked me (before asking my mom's permission) if I could get on a flight to Pittsburgh to appear on an educational children's TV show he was shooting there called Picture Pages.

I was nervous and asked him, "What if you don't like how I look in person?"

"Well then," he teased, "you'll just have to turn around, get back on the plane, and go home."

My parents thought it seemed like a great opportunity. After all, Bill Cosby was a personal friend of our neighbors, and one of the most beloved and respected people in the country, if not the world.

What could go wrong? He hadn't been named America's dad yet, but he was close to the age of my father. And I was just barely 16 years old.

So several days later, off I went to Pittsburgh. My career at that point consisted of lots of modeling, and a few commercials. Nothing crazy, but enough where I was now getting homeschooled which freed me up for auditions and photo shoots.

I arrived in Pittsburgh, and was met at the airport by Bill Cosby himself. Back then you could wait for arrivals right at the arrival gate, and there he was, holding my 8x10 black and white photo in his hands. When we made eye contact, he looked at my photo, then turned around started walking away. That was the beginning of our friendship. Him teasing me. Pretending he didn't like how I looked. It was funny. With his goofy, disarming smile, he seemed nice.

A chauffeur-driven car took us to the Pittsburgh Hilton, where he dropped me off. Bill was staying at a different hotel. The next day I was brought to set where I met back up with Cosby and the show's producer. They gave me a few lines to say, and it was all fairly easy and within my abilities. I met another girl there, a beautiful blonde student from UCLA. She seemed to know Bill. I never thought anything of it.

That night I was invited to the producer's house for dinner. It was a family style dinner. After we finished eating, after-dinner drinks were brought out and everyone had a drink. Everyone, that is, except for Cosby, who didn't touch anything. I had become a pretty heavy drinker by that point and I could handle my booze fairly well. We had a couple of cappuccinos spiked with Frangelico, the hazelnut-flavored liqueur. Soon I ditched the coffee and then single-handedly drank almost the entire bottle of the liquor. That I was underage didn't seem to faze anyone. My age didn't seem to matter to Cosby, the producer, or the producer's wife. And they all knew how old I was. As the evening wound down, I got into the car hired to take me back to the hotel. Cosby leaned in through the back window to kiss me goodnight. It started as a simple peck, but then he seemed to try to make it slightly more amorous. What was that all about?

When I got back up to my room at the hotel, the phone was ringing. It was Cosby. "I was just thinking of you," he said.

I didn't know how to respond so I simply told him good night and went to sleep.

The next morning on the set, he asked me if I felt like flying with him to Dallas the next day to attend his performance.

"Sure!" I said with the excitement of a16-year-old girl (which is what I was). "Why not? But I just need to ask my parents."

Cosby called them himself right then and there and told me they were fine with it. I saw the pretty girl from UCLA and said to her excitedly after talking to Cosby, "Are you going to Dallas with us, too?"

She shot me a stern look and silently walked away. I guess not.

The next day, before heading to the airport, Bill took me to Froggy's, a popular working-class Pittsburgh watering hole crammed with all sorts of local memorabilia. I started drinking rum and cokes while he and I made small talk about the trip we were about to take. Friends and well-wishers came and went from the table. Autographs and pictures taken. At one point a young waiter came up and instead of asking for Bill's autograph he asked for "seven digits" from me.

Bill responded harshly with "How about seven digits upside your head?"

Everyone seemed to laugh, but Bill had a sharp tone that was different for him. The waiter hustled away, realizing he made a grave mistake.

I wasn't carded or questioned at all. That I was with Bill Cosby seemed to make everything okay. Just like the night at the producer's home, I didn't see him touch a drop of alcohol. Little did I know Froggy's would eventually become a common spot for us to hang out while I got drunk over and over. Eventually, they'd even hang a picture of me on the wall, in honor of all the time I spent there with Cosby.

Then a limousine took us to the airport in Pittsburgh and out to the tarmac where the red and white Coca-Cola private Learjet was waiting for us. At that time Cosby was spokesman for Coca-Cola, among other popular brands.

Dona Speir

I had never seen anything like this before. You just pull right up to your private plane? No lines or waiting. People waiting there to help you. It was amazing. Drunk, I climbed aboard the jet and took it all in.

We were chasing the sun as we headed southwest, and an orange glow filled the cabin. Alone at the back of the plane, sitting next to each other, Cosby got more serious. At that point, I was so confused (and still a little drunk) that I just did what he wanted. I remember thinking that I just wanted to be a good girl. He was Bill Cosby. He had brought me there. He was the boss. I was just 16 years old. He silently eased my head toward his lap. I went back to my seat soon after as if nothing had even happened. We just stared out the windows, both silent. At one point I started to say something and he just hushed me like you would do to a child when you wanted them to go to sleep. Just saying "Shhhhhhh...."

We were met on the tarmac in Dallas by a long Cadillac convertible that had a big pair of shiny, polished Texas Longhorn antlers on the hood. From a 16 year old's perspective it was like something out of a cartoon. We were driven straight to the spectacular and historic resort hotel where we would be staying, the Mansion on Turtle Creek, a palatial estate built over a century ago. Presidents and royalty had all stayed there. And now, somehow, I would be staying there with Cosby. I wasn't sure what to expect, and I was nervous. After what had taken place on the plane, I had an idea about what his plan might be.

The magnificent suite just glittered, twinkled, and glowed. It was perfect, from the chandeliers to the high four-poster beds to the slightly overstuffed furniture that just enveloped you. Getting ready to leave for his performance, I made a mess of the bathroom putting on all of my makeup, like most teenage girls would've done. Everything was everywhere. Blue drugstore eye shadow, my curling iron, roll-on glossy lipsticks, and more, like a cosmetic bomb had gone off.

He came in and raised his eyebrows, shrugged, and said, "You did all that?"

I felt a little embarrassed and said "I'll take care of it later." I was just a teenage girl and I was very excited to be in such a beautiful, opulent place. At home I was raised sharing two bathrooms with eight people.

I put on my outfit for the evening: a pretty, turquoise Danskin leotard with a matching turquoise wrapped skirt below my knees; plastic Candies shoes, and matching turquoise earrings with green and purple

44

leaves. It was like playing grownup, getting all dressed up to tag along with Cosby.

The same car was waiting for us and whisked us off to the sold-out amphitheater where Cosby would be performing on what was a sultry, humid summer night. As we approached the venue at twilight, we started descending a ramp which would take us backstage and fans had lined up all alongside of it, waving excitedly and yelling. "There's Bill, there's Bill!" I heard them call out over and over.

He was up front with the driver and I was sitting in the back. It was exciting. It was like being in a parade.

Then all of a sudden out of that clamor came another voice. "To hell with Bill. Look at that girl in the back!" *Wow*, I thought. I had never been noticed like this out in public. I was a nobody. I had never been around a celebrity so I didn't know what this feeling was like. And it was invigorating.

Cosby performed that evening, and the thousands of people in attendance seemed to hang on his every joke and observation. After the show it was back in the car and back to the hotel. We arrived back up at our suite, and Cosby directed me to his bedroom even though my bags had been put in an adjoining room in the suite. It seemed obvious that this was where we would both be spending the night. He was 42. I was 16.

"What side of the bed do you want?" he asked me.

What side of the bed? I slept in a little twin bed at home. There were no "sides." I thought about what was happening and where I was. After a long pause I answered him. "I'll sleep on the side by the phone. In case my mom calls."

I don't remember much of what happened that night. I do remember Cosby went to play tennis in the morning and I was awoken by the sound of the door. A man with a package was standing there. He said it was for me from Bill. *A present? I never get presents. He sent me a present?* I was like a 10-year-old girl clapping and twirling.

I opened the package. It was a brown purse with two handles. It had LV all over it. It looked like his luggage. I had no idea what it was or why he had sent it to me. Just then the maids came in. One of the maids walked into the bathroom that I had gotten ready in the night before and picked up a boutonniere out of the trash. She picked it up and smelled it. Realizing it came from Bill's concert the night before, she put

Dona Speir

it in her pocket. All the while not realizing I was watching her while holding this silly brown bag. I saw her look into my bedroom to notice I hadn't slept there. She shook her head disapprovingly and then saw me, a very young underage girl standing there with a present in her hands. She slowly backed out of the suite. She knew.

Chapter Eight
What Groomers Do

There was nothing like traveling with Bill. It was the best. Beyond first class. I learned early on with him that there is a level reserved for people like him that most people don't even know exists. It's rare and somewhat royal. People who make other people money like this are exposed to it. I had gotten used to it by now. You didn't just get a suite. You got the entire top floor of a hotel if he was performing there. You got your own personal elevator. When he called me to visit him at the brand new Caesar's Hotel in Atlantic City, he invited my mom to go along. He had become part of my family. When he called my home looking for me he would chat with my mom for extended periods of time. This time he got on the phone and said "Mom, you're coming to Atlantic City with Dona." He called her "Mom" by now. She loved these trips. I think she was getting tired of vicariously living through me and enjoyed the chance to experience it herself.

Once we arrived, my mom was excited, but I'd seen it all before. Jaded at 16. There was a huge master suite on one side (his) and a few bedrooms on the other side connected by an oversized mutual living quarters. It was a complete home on the top of the hotel. One side of the suite was an entire glass wall facing the ocean. We always had the best views of wherever we were staying. Oceans, mountains, lakes—I only knew postcard perspectives. Cosby was absolute royalty to these resort hotels when he performed there, whether it was in Vegas, Reno, Tahoe, or Atlantic City.

I was this simple girl from a very middle class family. This was not normal to me. At least not at first. Months earlier, Bill and I had been lying on the floor together early one morning in his suite at the top of the Hilton in Las Vegas. We were having one of our "silly" conversations. We had these occasionally. Playful, fun little moments.

I had asked him what do you do with the little tips of the cigars that he bit off each time he lit one up, and he laughingly said while pointing, "Well, there's one, why don't you crawl over and grab it?" We were laughing pretty hard. And so we were both on the floor while I was crawling around picking them up, laughing and having fun. I liked that childlike side of him.

As we goofed around I asked him, "Bill, how much money do you make for each of these performances?"

"$100,000," he said casually.

And he sometimes did two shows a night. I remember thinking, *$100,000?* I flashed back to the days when I was a little girl and how on Saturdays I would sit with my dad at our dining room table. How he would write out his bills and let me lick the stamps and write the return addresses on the envelopes. I remember his payments for our home were $216 a month for our modest little house in Fountain Valley. So I couldn't even begin to understand $100,000 for one hour, let alone twice a night. But that's how much he was worth. He brought the people in. The casinos knew that, and so Cosby got whatever he wanted.

Entering the suite at Caesar's, my mom neatly unpacked her bags, and me, I flung my stuff around the room. That was always me. I was just footloose, fun, and free. I didn't care about making messes. I was like a tornado, always leaving a path of destruction in my wake.

And it was okay. I was a young teenage girl and Bill played into that role when my mom was around. It was the night, always at night, when things changed. When she would be asleep, and he would call for me.

Once settled into the suite, I did the first thing I always did whenever I checked into a hotel. I called up room service and ordered french fries and cheesecake. That was my teenage ritual, ordering those two items and then comparing which hotels prepared them the best. French fries and cheesecake were always on the top of my list. Unfortunately, drinking was becoming high on the list as well. Again, not around my mom when she would travel with us. I behaved around her, or at least gave that appearance. She had no idea how much I was drinking. But when it was just Bill and me, which was most of the time, I was drinking without discretion. It was like living a secret, double life—a price tag I would end up paying for many years to come. Looking back, I can see how I was torn between being a child and acting like an adult.

My mom, Bill, and a friend at dinner in Atlantic City.

After unpacking, Bill took us to dinner at a little place a few blocks away from the casino. He always had special places he wanted to share with us. As we strolled to the restaurant, a homeless man approached Bill and started giving him a hard time, asking for money. But then he recognized Bill immediately and his demeanor changed, and the two of them had a funny and spirited exchange before Bill gave him a $20 bill. He was very funny like that. He could mix it up with just about anybody, and, as famous as he was, he couldn't walk a few steps without being noticed, even by homeless people. That's just how recognizable he was. Whether it was the Jell-O commercials or Coca-Cola commercials, he was in people's living rooms almost every minute of every day. And the public adored him. They felt as if they knew him, and he had a way of putting anyone at ease. If he wanted to. Back then a Coca-Cola executive famously said, "The most believable personalities are God, Walter Cronkite, and Bill Cosby." And I don't think he was exaggerating that much.

After dinner, he sent us off to see the musical group Sister Sledge, who were performing nearby. I'd seen his act enough times. I could recite the entire thing and really didn't need to see it again. So rather than force me to sit through it, Bill would always make a phone call and I would be brought to the best seats in the house at another place in town, with an unlimited tab. So that night my mom and I went out on our own while Cosby went off and earned another six figures.

After Bill's shows, we would meet at some kind of funky, out-of-the-way jazz joint (unless he felt like hitting baccarat tables in the casino's private high roller rooms—another passion of his). He would sneak me in and seat me in the back, but immediately he would head to the stage. Bill played the drums, and loved sitting in with the bands in these smoke-filled, teeny clubs. The band would introduce him using a silly alias. Bill was in heaven.

I'll be honest: I didn't understand the music. And I hated listening to it. It made no sense and rarely had any recognizable melody. More importantly, this was an adult world, and I was just a kid. I usually sat by myself off to the side and I was bored. Bill was an adult. A middle-aged man. I was a kid. A kid pretending to be an adult. I pretended to be an adult a lot in those days. It's fun for a while. But then you end up sitting in smoke-filled rooms in the middle of the night, getting drunk alone in the dark.

It didn't matter to Bill if I cared for the music or not. I'm not even sure why he dragged me along. Was he trying to expose me to culture? Was he trying to entertain me? Really, what was the point? It was always a late night. 3:00 or 4:00 a.m. I never really understood. But that was his passion and I tagged along. But never ever to the baccarat table. Today the jazz club. Tomorrow? What would be next? But it never felt like he was letting me down. Instead it felt like I was letting *him* down. Like I wasn't living up to his fantasy of what I should be.

This night went pretty much like they all did. My mom went back to her suite to go to sleep, and Bill snuck me in to one of those tiny, nameless, underground jazz clubs. He excitedly hopped up on stage to play some drums while I sat bored in the corner, drinking rum and cokes, getting hammered. I never saw Bill touch a drop of alcohol, but he sure was seeing me drink a lot. I was tired and jet lagged from the flight the day before, but Bill didn't care. He was up there playing drums. Finally, at 4:00 a.m., he finally took me back to Caesar's. I wanted to go to bed, alone, to sleep, but that wasn't in the script. I knew what was expected of me and I wasn't about to act like a kid at 4:00 a.m.

I went back in to my suite, put on the big fluffy robe that hung in the bathroom closet, and quietly tiptoed over to Bill's bedroom while my mom slept. Normally I wouldn't have to be so careful, but whenever my mom or other family members were along for the trip, which had just started happening, I was very cautious. They had no idea I was sleeping with Bill Cosby. They were oblivious. He was family. And who wouldn't trust Bill Cosby?

I tiptoed across the mutual living area. It seemed like an eternity before I got to Bill's suite, hitting the furniture on the way over because I was so drunk by then. He was waiting for me at his doorway wearing the same robe. He had that smile on his face—not the goofy one where he rolls his eyes up into his head and purses his lips, but the one where he shows his teeth—his real smile. The room was dark, except for the pulsating lights of the casino that flickered just outside, barely illuminating the both of us. The room was silent.

In his gravelly voice he nodded and gently growled, "Yes," like I was being a good little girl as I walked into his arms. "Yes," he kept saying, "yes…" And at that moment I was. A good little girl.

Bill and I were together that night. And once again it was awkwardness at best. I was filled with shame and remorse. But I was always being reassured that he was there to take care of me. And his smile reaffirmed that I was a good girl. But then he would turn on me, and start telling me I couldn't do things right. What could you really know at 16, let alone being with a 42-year-old man? In my brain, sex was something you weren't even supposed to talk about, let alone do. As a friend and mentor, I adored Bill. He was generous and caring with his time and generosity. As a lover, though, he wasn't just an old man to me—he also made me feel confused, unworthy, and insecure.

"You need to learn how to kiss," he would say to me in bed. "You don't kiss right."

No one had ever taught me any of this stuff. I was just making it up as I went along. What sort of middle-aged man says that to a teenage girl? Fuck, this was getting confusing. In fact, not only did I not know how to kiss, I didn't know how to dress, or act.

Dona Speir

When it was over, I snuck back to my room and crashed for what little of the night was left. I was in over my head.

I didn't need a lot of sleep. A lot of teenagers will sleep all hours but that wasn't me. I could wake up with just a few hours of sleep, and, no matter how much I drank the night before, I was rarely hung over. Being with Bill was definitely helping me increase my tolerance.

I wish I'd had the ability to think about what the drinking was doing to me. I had no idea what alcoholism was or how much of my life the disease would eventually claim. What kind of an adult keeps a bottomless booze tab running for his underage girlfriend, watching night after night as she drinks excessively? Was it just about sex? He could have gotten that anyplace. Was it about control?

Later that morning, the maids had already pulled back the blackout curtains from the night before, and when I opened the drapes it was like seeing Disneyland. My heart soared. So many young people—bustling, running, and playing around the boardwalk. It was like seeing color for the first time after the previous night of a black and white world. That's where I wanted to be. Down there on the warm sand. I was slipping away emotionally but part of my spirit was strong and it was still calling me. I was a southern California girl who would ride her beach cruiser bicycle to the beach every day that I could. That life was becoming a distant memory, and, all of a sudden, I missed it. I could see the boardwalk and the amusement park. It looked like who I really was. I knew I was changing. I knew I had secrets and I was living through battles. I was slowly dying inside. My inner conflicts were heavy. As I looked down there I felt sad, but there was action and activity. There was life and I really needed to be down there. My youth was waiting for me.

My mom was in no rush to leave the suite and so I slipped into my bathing suit and quickly made like a gazelle over to Bill's room (at that age I was always leaping around with tons of energy).

I bounded into his room unannounced and blared, "I'm going down to the beach!"

"Hold on, young lady," he said sternly to me. It was strange how he spoke to me like a father figure sometimes. As if I had never gone to the beach or as if my own parent was not even in the next suite over. "I'm taking you down myself," he intoned seriously.

52

He was dressed for a noontime tennis match, which he loved doing as much as playing the drums, but before hitting the courts he was going to personally escort me down to the beach. I was not happy.

That was not the Bill Cosby I had gotten to know over the last year or so. The man I knew would never risk being out in such a public place during such a busy time. A Saturday morning on the jam-packed boardwalk at Atlantic City? Shit, there was no way he wasn't going to get mobbed by fans and he knew that. But for some reason, a short while later we were in the private elevator and headed out toward the private beach area that the hotel maintained. This was crazy. There was no way he was not going to get recognized.

"Are you sure you want to do this?" I asked him. "I can get down there by myself. I'm fine." It was a production and I just wanted to go. Things had changed.

But he dismissed me. "I'm taking you down there. Let's go."

From the second we set foot out in the bright summer sunshine, it started.

"Bill! Bill!"

"Look, it's Bill Cosby!"

"Can you take a picture with us?"

"I love your Coke commercials!"

It was an instant train wreck, attracting more attention the bigger the crowd became.

What was he thinking? It's not that we never went out in public, but we were discreet, and always careful to avoid the masses for just this reason. People went crazy when they saw him.

Tourists sucking down their hot dogs and ice cream couldn't believe they were seeing one of the most famous men on the planet walking amongst them. Bill had a funny way of dealing with the public for those times when word got out he was there. He didn't stop to talk, or he would have been easily mobbed. Instead he had a system where he moved quickly, making his faces and using his hand signals, pointing and laughing raising his eyebrows. It was like he was acting out a silent movie, but always moving quickly.

I'll never forget the first time I saw him work this "system" It was a few months earlier while driving through Beverly Hills with him in his root-beer-brown Mercedes sedan. Bill was at the wheel, showing me one of his houses he had lived in years ago, and, when he wasn't paying attention and ran a stop sign, he almost hit a carload of ladies that had to slam on their brakes in the middle of the street as we drove through. That was the first time I saw the silent Bill Cosby charm that would always get him out of trouble. He did one of his silly faces, eyes wide open, raised his arms in mock shock, and I saw the lady in the passenger seat mouth the words "Bill Cosby." They were all thrilled and surprised and we just kept driving.

On the boardwalk that day, people were no less delighted at the little show they were getting, unaware that Bill was just doing what he had to do to maneuver through the situation. A total master of deflection.

Once we were able to get to the private space on the beach that was part of Caesar's, things calmed down quickly and Bill got down to business. I remember the faces of the cabana boys when they saw Bill walking with me. They couldn't believe it was him, *the* Bill Cosby, with a curvy, sexy young blonde in tow.

Bill approached one of them, a cute beach boy who might have been pushing 20. "Look," he said to the kid, all business, "I want you to take care of this young lady today, do you understand?"

Wide eyed, the kid just nodded and stared as Cosby laid down the law.

"You get her what she wants. If she wants to eat, you get her food. If she wants to swim, you swim. You keep an eye on her at all times. Anything she wants you make sure she has it. Got it? Good!"

The kid nodded vigorously as Cosby pressed what looked like a couple of twenties into his hand. "But that's all you're to do," Cosby admonished. "You see that she gets what she wants, keep your eyes on her and see to it and that nobody hassles her, got it? That means you, too." And then came that disarming Cosby laugh. He might have tried to act like he was joking around, but I knew he was serious. He made his point.

The kid got the message: I was spoken for. And even though I could feel the eyes of some of the other cabana boys, they all seemed to get the message, too. I was off limits. "Yes sir, I completely understand and you have nothing to worry about, sir." Then the kid quickly fetched me a towel, lounge chair, cabana—and anything else he could manage to tuck under his arms.

It was like the treatment I would get in nightclubs, restaurants, and other places where Bill made the arrangements. Always the best, and I was always the most attended-to girl in the room. But this scene also felt different. The waiters and maître d's were never addressed as if they were any kind of threat. Maybe Bill was sensing my desire to just be a California beach girl for a day and so the cabana boys presented a new sort of challenge. Young, attractive, tan, and shirtless—maybe he thought they might give him a run for his money.

Bill asked me if I needed anything else, I told him I was fine, and then, in his fancy white tennis clothes, he turned and walked away, giving me a sharp, slightly-baleful glance over his shoulder. He wasn't any more than 30 feet from me when I saw people again starting to approach him, and, just like he had on the walk out, he worked his way through the crowd quickly and efficiently on the way to his tennis game. The last thing I saw was the sun glint off his showy platinum I.D. bracelet. The one that had his wife's name, "Camille," on it. They had been married since 1964. The year I was born.

Lying on the beach, the wind drifting out into the blue-green ocean, life had become so confusing and twisted. I now had absolutely nothing in common with my high school friends back in Fountain Valley. My old girlfriends might've had a date on a Saturday night to go to a movie or something. Me, I was usually heading off to Las Vegas or Reno or Tahoe to be with Bill. I might be at a fancy restaurant or exclusive club. The best seat at a popular show. But wherever it was, my drinking was escalating. I was beginning to cross a line. Still, my world was exciting and Bill really seemed to care about me. He listened to me. I could call him any time and he would talk to me. I thought, *how could something so wrong be so right? And how could something that felt so right... be so wrong?* It was at this time I began to feel isolated and alone. There really was no one I could turn to except for Bill. When I would act out in fits of anger at home because of confusion over this situation, my mom would say, "Maybe you should call Bill—he always seems to help you, honey." Not knowing he was the main reason I was acting out, along with what Jack had done to me.

I had feelings of "normalcy" that day—of freedom—at least for every 20 minutes or so until the blonde kid made his rounds on me (not unlike an eager cocktail waitress looking to refill drinks). As I went into the Atlantic Ocean for the first time in my life, I was surprised at how

55

warm the water was. I was swimming in what little surf they had, and as I turned around, there was the blonde kid right on my tail—even in the water. It wasn't as if Bill paid him to be friends with me—he paid to make sure I didn't have friends. That was unless he approved of the when and where. The one time I did bring a friend with me to Pittsburg it was a disaster. He thought I had told her, which I didn't. He wanted to immediately send her home. I didn't live in his world where this behavior was normal.

How does a white teenage girl explain she got herself involved with an African-American man 26 years her senior and they're romantically involved? In 1980, you didn't. I was used to keeping secrets by then. Besides, I already believed I was damaged goods. Playing grown-up at this level takes its toll pretty fast. I did not have the tools to handle such an adult situation. I was not emotionally equipped to be a grown-up but you could not have told me different. The fancy places and things I'd been experiencing were just bows wrapped on an empty box.

It felt good to lie on the beach. It reminded me of the days on Huntington Beach with my high school friends. When times were easier. I just closed my eyes and listened to the sounds of kids laughing and people having fun up on the boardwalk.

At one point, the cabana guy mustered up the courage to ask me, "So how do you know Mr. Cosby?"

"We work together," I told him.

Of course, that wasn't really true. Sure, he had included me in a few of his episodes of Picture Pages and he would try and help me push my career along by calling my agent, introducing me to people in the industry, and arranging for photo shoots. I mean, he acted like he was helping. Who really knows.

But saying that we "worked" together was a long shot. I could have been honest with the kid. I could have said that Bill and I simply had a deeply personal relationship. I could have told him there were many days I would fight with my parents and then call Bill, crying. I would reach him in his dressing room right before he went on stage. I would be sobbing over teenage troubles. He always took my calls. By the end of our conversation we both would be laughing hysterically, either ending it with plans to get together or joking about me calling him and sobbing right before he had to go on stage to make people laugh. That was always our joke, that my timing was never good.

I could have told the kid all that. But of course I didn't. My life had become a cabinet of dark and forbidden secrets. Lies, lies, and more lies, and always covering my trails. Empty. Without purpose.

In the afternoon, I had a surprise. My mom came down from the suite to join me, and she and I explored the boardwalk together. We took the little train down to one end and walked back. It was as if we were recapturing a piece of my wasted, jagged youth, trying together to make up for lost time. It was wonderful. My mom was excited to spend innocent time like this with her teenage daughter. I know she had started to sense that I was slipping away. It had begun with the photographer back in Fountain Valley. She was happy that I was acting my age for once. I had grown up in such a few short years and she didn't know why. I was a mystery to her. So I liked seeing my mom smile like she was, looking at me the way she did when I was a little girl.

We were a lot alike. No matter how old we got, total kids at heart. That was my mom and that's me today. Never fully growing up. We ate corn dogs and cotton candy, went to a fortuneteller's booth, and rode pedicabs. I stopped at a stall where soft, colorful toy critters hung from hooks and I bought a stuffed monkey. I acted silly. It was the best day I had had with my mom in years and I could see in her eyes how much she appreciated it. It was the last time she would see me like this for a long time.

Atlantic City on the boardwalk with my stuffed monkey.
This was taken by my mom.

I can't even imagine what my mom was really thinking at this time. I know trips like this were exciting to her, and I know she trusted Bill.

Dona Speir

Everybody trusted Bill. But she had to be wondering inside what might really be going on. There had to be questions she had. Not so much about Bill and me, because that was covered up so well. But about my behavior, how fast I was growing up, and how much I was changing before her eyes. It really helped that I was a working model without Bill's help.

I'm sure people will now wonder: how could my mom not possibly know what was happening? How could she not know I was in an intimate relationship with Bill Cosby? But I'm convinced she was oblivious. Everyone was oblivious. I mean, in 1980, who would ever imagine that their lily-white 16-year-old daughter would be sleeping with a 42-year-old married Black man? Even if she was a budding wild child? And I know my father would have killed him had he known. My father was proud and protective. Bill appeared to be doing so much for my career, mentoring me all the time, lighting my future path, that it was easy for everyone to buy into. I wasn't about to say anything. I felt like *I* was the one in the wrong, not him. I was being a bad girl. I *was* a bad girl. So I had to keep that hidden. If my parents were alive today, I would not be sharing any of this. It would have died with me. I never would have had the heart to put my parents in the position of knowing this had happened on their watch. It was my fault, not theirs. That's how I felt then. It was instilled in my head for so many years that, even as a child, I should have known better.

After our fun day, back up in the suite, I shared with Bill what my mom and I did that afternoon. I was hoping he'd be happy for us. He was a parent and maybe he'd appreciate that time we spent together. It was just the opposite, though. He seemed put off, especially with the fortuneteller. I tried to explain that it had just been for fun and showed him all the trinkets I had collected. But he was borderline dismissive. This all seemed beneath him. He made faces that seemed to express disapproval and he shook his head. All of my little treasures my mom and I collected had no value to him. I felt embarrassed and my heart sank. It wasn't good enough and neither was I. One more time I felt shame. All of a sudden I became very sad. I felt I could never make anyone happy. I was caught up in this crazy world where no one was really happy with me, or my age, or anything I did. I didn't really fit in. My own skin was tight and increasingly uncomfortable. And I had all but ditched my previous life. If this one didn't work out, I wasn't sure what was left for me. At 16 I needed a drink. Anything to change the way I felt and to please the people around me. This was his way of controlling my relationship with my mother and creating a wall between her and me. I had to make a choice.

Bill had showered and was getting ready for his performance that night. As he got dressed he told us, "Tonight I've made arrangements for mom and you to see someone special: Johnny Mathis."

Oh brother. Back to the old person's world. Was Bill trying to torture me? And, oh yeah, again, why did he now always call *my* mom "Mom"?

Getting rid of that stinky cigar right before
going on stage. I hated those things.

I didn't have the heart to tell him that the last place in the world I wanted to be that night was at a Johnny Mathis concert. After his disapproval of today's actions, I needed to make it up to him. I could see how disappointed he was in me. How miffed he was at me. It was like jazz to me. I knew I would be bored out of my teenaged skull. After my time spent on the boardwalk that day, I was starting to itch for something more normal in my life: all of the things a 17-year-old does. The routine was starting to get to me.

My mom, of course, was excited. She loved Johnny Mathis. That was *her* music. Maybe that was it. Maybe Bill was trying to impress her even more so that he could continue seeing me without any questions or suspicions. Maybe what I thought, at least when my mom was around, didn't really matter at all. That was probably part of his whole "grooming" process. Either way, that night we got dressed up and off we went to see Johnny Mathis. We got there, I gave my name, and of course we were quickly escorted to the best table in the house. The ceiling at the casino club seemed low to me, and everything was lit in a starlight blue. It was cramped and claustrophobic. The whole scene reminded me of the Dean Martin show my parents used to watch in black and white on TV: all tuxedoes, cigarettes, and stale jokes. Once again, a way to separate my mother from me. Make him look like a hero to her, make me come running to him.

As the concert wore on, I sat there, getting more bored, disinterested, and edgy. This was hell. Johnny Mathis was elegant and classy and all that. But I couldn't've cared less. The music was boring to me. The audience was boring. The entire scene could've put me to sleep. All of a sudden I was looking forward to meeting Bill in some sketchy little jazz club so he could play drums while I drank before we went home and went to bed. Pretty sad when that becomes the escape you look forward to.

Bill Cosby was smart. He knew that the best way to protect his time with me was to ingratiate himself with my family. That's what groomers do. That's with the photographer had done just a couple of years earlier: made friends with my family to develop a bond of trust. Once you have the parents on your side, you can get away with a lot more. Bill Cosby was a master at this. He knew how to not just wine and dine my family but also how to express concern and share the fact that he was trying to help me with my career. He had called my agents in Hollywood, made appointments with his agents, spent hours on the phone soothing over parental arguments and more, always offering to fly me up to where he was when things were too heated at home. What parent would not love that? There were many lavish vacations where Cosby would fly my entire family to Atlantic City or Tahoe or Las Vegas and put them up in a four-star suite, taking them out on the town and letting them come and enjoy his performances. That provided all of the trust so that he could secretly spend intimate time with me.

This had become the new normal.

I remember this one time in particular, my parents and sisters all had enormous suites all next to each other. They were under the main suite at the Hilton in Las Vegas. They were enormous. I can't remember how many but there were at least four of them. There we were, on a small family vacation, living like royalty in Las Vegas. I have no idea what in the world everyone was doing. I wasn't even old enough to be in the casino. We would all be hanging backstage in his dressing room, having dinner with him before the show, or afterwards having drinks with him. They were always allowed to visit Bill Harrah (the famous casino owner) at home if I was with him in Nevada or anywhere else for that matter. He took us to the Tonight Show when he co-hosted and we got to meet Tina Turner. He sent my sister flowers when she was in the hospital. He did everything for everyone, these total strangers, just to build a façade so that he could continue his relationship with me.

Once, Bill paid a limousine driver for days on end to squire my mother and me around New York City. He wanted us to see everything and eat at different restaurants every night, all of his favorites haunts, from Italian to Chinese cuisine. He was always making sure everything was taken care of in advance. On the career front, he arranged for me to shoot a Coca-Cola ad, working for the McCann Erickson agency like he did. What made Cosby extra dangerous was the fact that he had the money to really impress my family. We came from simple means and all of a sudden we were living like A-listers, all thanks to America's Dad. A groomer is dangerous enough. A wealthy groomer is another form of evil altogether, because they have the means to create entirely new worlds for people, completely warping all senses of reality to create totally artificial levels of trust.

Sitting in Cosby's nightshirts was an every night occurrence.

Chapter Nine
A Teenaged Drug Runner

By now I was 17. I was modeling and had slowed down with the drugs and drinking. Though involved with Cosby, I was still trying to shake the thoughts of the abuse from Jack. But there really was no escaping it. It haunted me through and through. It was so ingrained in me and yet I had never spoken about it to anyone. I was struggling, but I used to go to Disneyland a lot at night to go dancing with girlfriends and unwind. During my time at home away from Cosby, I met Rick one night at Disneyland. It was the only place minors could go to dance. Also, part of me still yearned to be a kid. I think that was Rick's quest too. Though he was a bit shifty, like myself, he loved to watch the Sunday night Disney movies on TV. He loved his little mutt dogs and his mom. He was more like me than I wanted to admit. He was a misfit and an outcast. Though somewhere I sensed he had been wounded more than I could ever imagine. That's what we had in common. Secret pain was something to bond over.

Rick was different from anyone I had ever met. He was a hustler. Fast talker, flashy, and not particularly well spoken. But funny. He was a funny guy. He was also a few years older than me and somewhat good looking. The night I first met him, he gave me a dozen or more Thai sticks. Thai sticks were a popular form of weed back in the day that were tied around a stick and were very potent. However, I had given up smoking weed by then, so the next day I sold them and made some extra cash. When we left Disneyland and walked out to his car, I was taken aback. A very new and flashy Porsche. What did this guy do for a living? We parted that night after hanging out, but that was it. No phone numbers, no nothing—just a nice night talking.

Several months later I ran into him again at Knott's Berry farm. Once again I was there to dance to a well-known band from Orange County. Rick suggested my girlfriend and I follow him up to LA to another dance club for minors and we did. He seemed to know everyone in LA. He introduced us to some fun people and we ended up going over to some other person's home, but then I didn't see him for the rest of the night.

I had given Rick my number and he called to ask me out on a date. I accepted. My mom was not impressed when he arrived. He wasn't like my first boyfriend (or any of the other occasional boys) I had dated. When he came to pick me up, I knew something was off. He wasn't in his flashy Porsche. He was in a semi-beat-up old car. As we walked out he didn't open my car door either. Two red flags. I liked some manners and even a bit of chivalry. I wish I had run then.

My parents had serious issues with him. He wasn't in school and still lived in his parents' home in San Clemente, even though he was old enough to be out on his own. It was a nice home that was close to the beach. His sister lived in the lower house, and, like with most houses in San Clemente, you had to walk up the stairs to get to the main house. There was a pretty ocean view. After our first date, it was apparent to me that Rick did not inherit his money, as he had explained to me over dinner. He was simply a large-scale marijuana dealer, dealing out of his parents' home. Ironic when you stop to consider that his father was once a prison guard.

He had always told me he dealt weed because dealing cocaine would put you in prison and you then would have to contend with absolutely crazy people. He felt that dealing weed was a lot less dangerous. Was this the relationship I needed at this time in my life? No. Did I dive in headfirst without even considering any of the obvious consequences? Of course I did. My common sense compass has been destroyed long before.

It wasn't long after Rick and I were together that things slowly got out of control. Not that I wasn't already out of control. I had just buried it for a while. Seems that way, since I had a reprieve off of the hard drugs and I hadn't ended up in the emergency room or psychiatric ward in a while. I never had a cocaine problem. In fact, I always disliked any type of speed. It was the early '80s and it was slowly infiltrating the mainstream and, a lot of times, when it was offered, I would turn it down. It just wasn't my thing. The same with Rick. He seemed to have a lot of it, but it was more for other people who partied around us and bought his drugs. We drank fancy champagne and a few beers, but really didn't do hard drugs. We spent a lot of time like normal kids. Dancing, and going to parties. We fished together and waterskied with friends. He was different but fun. Then ever so gradually Rick opened up his world of drug dealing to me. I became an assistant, and an accomplice. The next reckless and wild phase of my young life was about to kick in.

Rick and I would sit up all night counting hundreds of thousands of dollars, rubber-banding it and duffel-bagging everything. This house always reeking of weed. It was a serious operation. Scales and trash bags everywhere. When we weren't delivering drugs or picking up money, we would go trap shooting at the range or see movies. I remember one day there was a bunny running around the trap field. Rick was afraid it would get killed so he stopped the shooters and trapped it. The next thing you know, he's got a wild bunny living in a cage in his room at his parents' place. He was very childlike in so many ways. It was always something out of a crazy movie.

When a shipment of weed came in, we would sit up all night breaking up the "bushels." Since I didn't smoke weed, it really had no value to me. Breaking up 500 pounds of weed was something we did probably once every few weeks. Little by little cocaine became the fuel of choice. The weed made a mess and smelled awful. But no matter, we broke it down and packaged it up for buyers. Laughing about what a mess it made. Out would go the deliveries and in would roll the money. Up all night again counting was our routine, doing a few more lines here and there, having a few drinks. We needed to keep things as under control as we could to make sure we had all our bases covered.

On one particular shipment, Rick's father had had enough. He was a big scary man who ran an insurance company in town. He knew what was going on and finally snapped. It was mid-morning and I had just pulled up to the house and a shipment of hash had come in. The packages were wrapped in tight yellow cellophane with a stamp from Turkey. They were shaped like wooden house shingles, weighting a kilo each, and we had way too many of them. Way.

When I parked on the street, I heard his dad screaming at the top of his lungs about how he was sick and tired of his drug dealing. "Richard, this shit is over! You're going to get us all thrown in jail, you little prick! Your mother and I have had it!" His father was flinging these shingles of hash over the front balcony onto the driveway.

I had hidden under the awning of the balcony, running out and gathering up the hash so that we could still sell it. Trying to hide from this huge man and hide the drugs from the neighbors. It was a three-ring circus. By the time the tirade was over, I was sitting under the balcony with approximately 220 pounds of hash in a pile. It resembled a really bad game show.

It was time to move out.

Rick rented a house, but I did not move in right away. Friends came and went but deals weren't done in the house. By now, Rick was renting venues to throw parties like his friends did in LA. The venues were total dens of drug abuse. Cocaine was being snorted on tables and in every bathroom. He was charging money at the door, and was raking in a small fortune. He soon bought a boat and we would take it out to fish or waterski. Money was flying in, and, by now, so was the cocaine. We weren't quite dealing the white powder, at least not on the scale of the hash or weed. I was now making some drug runs, just drop-offs and pick-ups. No big deal. At least not in my mind. Around 10–20 pounds here and there. Compared to what he was doing, it was nothing.

I had started to catch Rick lying to me about things and it was driving me crazy. I was beginning to get gaslighted by him. It was Easter Sunday and he said he was going fishing and that he would be right back. He never returned and left me alone at his house with no car keys. After many hours I turned on the TV news and there he was with his best friend in Palm Springs with a couple girls in the car. It was Spring Break and he was down there with all the college girls! I took a large amount of hash and hitchhiked to my parents' house. To spite Rick, I gave it to the guy who gave me the ride—a half-pound of hash just to get even! I broke up with him that day. I was done. But he was not done with me. I was modeling at a convention a week later when Rick showed up with a beautiful necklace, begging for forgiveness. I took him back. This was the beginning of what would be yet another spiral into hell. The occasional line or two of cocaine was now becoming way more than a habit. One day at a shoot, I did a few lines on the back of a toilet. I came out and came alive in front of the camera. Wow. How well I worked. It was spectacular. The shots were unreal. I found heaven. I could work, and perform on blow. It wasn't like alcohol. This was magic.

I was doing my share of cocaine by now and he was giving me bindles (little envelopes) of my own. We would often go out to dinner with friends in Laguna Beach. After dinner one night I went to light a cigarette when the waiter came by and lit it for me. The entire cigarette went up in flames. I had stuffed half the cigarette with blow and the entire cigarette had ignited. Our table broke out into laughter. Seems I had forgotten what I had done. The waiter continued to light the cigarette and the odor traveled through the restaurant. It was blatant. I was beginning not to care where or when I did cocaine. The guys had just done lines on the bread plates before we paid the bill. We were becoming reckless and we didn't care. Defiant. We all laughed and left the restaurant. My weight was slowly going down and I was beginning to get a reputation with my agents as difficult. That's what coke does to you.

I was not doing coke every day but it was getting close. I was beginning to get paranoid. Rick was now cutting me off from "the stuff," as he called it. He knew I was becoming a liability. I was beginning to steal cash from the money-counting marathons, shorting the stacks as we rubber-banded them together. He started searching my bags for "the stuff," which meant I had to hide it. When I went over his house I would stop at the gas station on the corner and give the attendant my blow and a few ounces of weed to hold my stash until I came back in half an hour. There were always a few pounds of weed left in the carpet. I would pick it up with the broom and throw it in a trash bag. We would disperse it through the various pounds of weed. It was known as shake—the garbage to be mixed with the good. I really didn't think it was obvious that I was on blow, but, looking back, the fact that I gave Rick a written list of license plates that I swore were following me down the freeway gave away the fact that I was paranoid. I was a mess. He just could never find "the stuff" on me, and I made sure of that.

When I didn't have the money to buy drugs, it meant it was time for drastic measures. There was usually coke in the safe or enough cash to buy some. If all else failed, I could trade some weed. The weed trade was a pain in the ass. At different times I would weigh out one-pound bags and hide them in various places in Rick's new house. No one ever noticed if one or two pounds went missing here or there. We would lose that much in the carpeting. So when I didn't have cash to buy coke, off I went trading a pound of weed for a gram or two of cocaine. It was easiest that way. No haggling, I got my drugs, and, since I didn't smoke weed, it really had no monetary value to me. Just crap that I had to clean up off the floor.

The problem with the one-pound bags was I constantly forgot where I hid them. Some in the attic, some in boxes in the garage, some in trunks, some I don't think I ever found. I accidentally left three of them in the trunk of my father's car for over a week while he carpooled back and forth to work with his three carpool mates. Then, four years later when I was having a garage sale, I found two one-pound disintegrated bags in some glassware that had been out for sale. It was crazy.

I didn't have the combination to the safe in the house (for very good reasons), or so he thought. I had watched over his shoulder enough to get all three numbers and then I figured out the sequence. The cash in the safe was always good and I would blame him for miscounting, or suggest that his friends could possibly know the combo, or that Rick was drunk and spent it. All deflection and lies. The missing coke was always a problem because I was usually high when he found it missing.

When things couldn't get worse, they did. Snorting cocaine wasn't working as well as it always had and then Rick introduced me to freebasing, which was basically smoking cocaine in its purest form. No one really did that then. Doing it back then was as bad as shooting heroin. You were considered a real drug addict if you did that. I loved it the first time I did it. Rick had been bugging me to marry him. It was the stupidest idea he had ever had. I was 17. I was freebasing, seeing Cosby, snorting blow, trying to model, selling weed, all the while keeping everything a secret. Juggling 20 different lives. Cosby didn't know about Rick; Rick didn't know about Cosby. I did drugs with Rick. Not with Cosby. Every couple of months when Cosby invited me out on the road, I'd usually go. My mom didn't know about the cocaine or my relationship with Cosby. My parents hated Rick (what parents wouldn't?) and I was more out of control than ever.

Rick and I were asleep one night when I awoke and once again he wasn't there. I called around and found him at one of his friends' houses smoking base cocaine. I put on my clothes and literally ran four miles in the middle of the night so I could smoke base with them. When I got to the house, everyone was out of their minds and I couldn't wait. They were running low on supplies and I had to go find a 7-Eleven to buy baking soda to cook more. It was a ritual: sweating, grinding your teeth, and cooking up coke.

So it began. My new world of basing. Or "playing baseball," they would sometimes call it. Back at Rick's house, sheets went up on the windows, and around this time someone broke into the house. We had just delivered all funds and there were only about 20 pounds lying around. I think they only stole a shotgun. But it was getting dicey. Once again, Rick had left me alone at the house without car keys, and I took a bat and broke the windows on his cars. We had started physically fighting now because he had cut me off of all drugs. He had started hiding the cocaine from me. Now people were coming up to our windows in the middle of the night, tapping on them to buy cocaine. About this time, I came up with a brilliant idea. I would grind up Valium in the coke grinder and put it in Rick's drink to knock him out cold while I stole the drugs.

"Something's wrong," he said after a few drinks into the night.

It's amazing I didn't kill him.

In the daylight, I was driving large quantities of pot down the freeway. I would have 250 pounds or so in Hefty trash bags in the bed of my truck without a camper shell. A duffel bag under my seat with anywhere from $20,000–$30,000. I had become delusional. I believed, since I was this nice girl from Fountain Valley, that if I got pulled over, the cops would let me go.

Garden Grove was about 30 miles up the freeway. I was making this run almost every Sunday afternoon to drop off drugs, but at one particular house there was something else going on: a counterfeit scheme. They were inside bleaching $1 bills on one side and getting ready to print on the other. Blank bills were clipped up all over the kitchen. I would leave with a paper bag full of money and go to the truck with Hefty bags of weed in the back. Kind of like a gardener.

I was using so much cocaine that I had to find my own connections. I couldn't use Rick's because he threatened to cut them off of weed if they sold to me. Selling weed was a big source of income to a lot of people we knew. My weight was dwindling rapidly, especially since I was freebasing as often as I could. My agents had pretty much stopped calling because I couldn't show up. When I went home to my parents, it was usually to come down off drugs and I was agitated and strung out. I was fighting with them.

Then mom would say something like, "Maybe you should talk to Bill." *FUCK.* "Bill's been calling." *FUCK.* "He has helped you with a lot of stuff, honey." *FUCK.*

FUCK FUCK FUCK FUCK FUCK.

I know it sounds crazy, but somehow in the middle of all of this drug dealing I was still able to work in little trips with Bill Cosby. He would call me, I would drop everything, and go hop on a private plane to wherever he was. I was young, free to do what I wanted, and had all of the time and energy in the world. High school? No problem. I became a drop out. I started out living a double life, which then became a triple life, and may have even been worse than that at times. My parents and siblings barely kept track of me. I had created my own worlds away from them and honestly I think everybody was relieved that they didn't have to deal with me on any sort of regular basis. I was just too big a handful. Like I've said, I believe I was born predisposed to certain addictive behaviors. But there's also zero doubt in my mind that what Jack did to me set me off on a course of pain and destruction that I doubt I would've ever discovered on my own. Sexual abuse causes damage that can and will last forever.

Meanwhile, back in Huntington Beach, the craziness continued. I found three new drug connections, two of them in Huntington Beach. One was downtown and the other in a nearby barrio. (I have no idea how I got connected with them, but one of the connections was the husband of Ashley. Jack's daughter. Small world, and, needless to say, she was less than thrilled to see me. I'm not even sure why; who knew what she knew.) The third connection was back in Garden Grove. Rick and I by now were extremely volatile and getting into physical altercations regularly. One night, he was arrested after I called the police on him for beating me at his home. We were probably fighting over drugs. I can't even remember. I went back to my parents' home, which was much closer to my two new Huntington Beach connections. One night, while drinking beer at Ashley's house, I called Rick. He had been begging me to get back together. Begging to marry me. Anything to get back together. I had had six beers and told him to pick me up. I'm not even sure why.

On April 27th, 1982, Rick and I got married at Chapel of the Bells in Vegas. You read that right. I wore a pair of dolphin shorts, a braless tank shirt, and Nike tennis shoes. I was two months past my 18th birthday.

I moved in with Rick and the next day called Cosby and told him I got married.

"What?" he said, with a slight chuckle. "What are you up to now? Dona, Dona, Dona."

I could tell he wasn't taking me seriously. "I can't see you anymore," I told him.

"Well, okay, we'll just see, okay, Dona?"

I was actually relieved.

The marriage would be the longest 63 days of my life.

Dona Speir

Chapter Ten
Praying For Death

I moved in with Rick right after we got married. I was practically living at his place anyway. My parents were so incredibly disappointed and so was everyone I knew. My parents had high hopes for me, as they did for all their children, but they had become discouraged. I had thrown my life away, but I didn't give a fuck. I was so strung out by now. Rick was becoming so controlling with the drugs, and when he decided it was ok, he and I would hunker down and spend days smoking "The stuff." When we did that, my ears would start ringing, my pores sweating, and there would be long nights of staring at each other, hearing imaginary noises. Him swearing that I had just stolen big rocks of coke from him. Me on the floor crawling around looking for pieces I might have dropped, putting anything that resembled cocaine in the pipe and smoking it. The desperate paranoia, the maniacal hunger for cocaine, and the sick, sordid relationship all made for an endless nightmare. The coming down was especially horrible.

He would blame me every time. "You made me do this! You made me smoke for days!"

He had a way of shaming me for everything. But then again, every man I had now known would either verbally, emotionally, or physically beat me up.

The shaming had actually started not long after we first got together. Rick had this girlfriend at one time named Lisa who lived in Beverly Hills. He was constantly comparing me to her, saying things like, "Lisa wouldn't have done that, Lisa wouldn't have worn this, Lisa's family has so much money, her father is a surgeon you know, you'll never amount to anything." Nice stuff like that.

I never got to meet her. But from what I heard, Lisa was beautiful and always acted like a lady. From what I understood, her father was indeed a doctor in Beverly Hills and that's what Rick truly wanted. Not me but her. I was always made to feel like second place. He was still in contact with her and threw her at me whenever I didn't do what he wanted or he felt bad about himself. He was always saying to me, "You can take the girl out of the gutter, but you can't take the gutter out of the girl."

It was never ending.

So, when we would come down off of a three-day bender, somehow, he would take it out on me. It was his way of justifying what he had done. "Look at you, you look like shit, you would never make it in Beverly Hills."

It was always the price tag I would pay for marrying the coke dealer. For selling my soul for drugs. For doing what I needed to do to stay high. To get away from myself, all the while lying by saying we were a real couple.

One day after about a month of living together and marriage, Rick struck me hard. We were in the living room and we had been arguing. We had already crossed the line numerous times with physical violence. One time it happened in front of his older brother, who did nothing to help me. He just sat there and let Rick beat me up. This time though, it really got out of control. I never saw this one coming. I got hit across the face quickly and bluntly. Without words or incident, that was it. I had had enough. I grabbed a few things and took off running. I grabbed the truck, and screamed out of there for good. Strung out or not, I would not take the physical abuse anymore. I was down to about 105 pounds by then and my hair had become stringy. I was starting to disintegrate from the drugs. And so I ran, and fast.

With my addiction still incredibly active, I crashed at my parents' house once again. I had nowhere else to go and no way of supporting myself. Back in the room with the rainbow wallpaper. It became my personal hell. I was agitated. Looking back, it's amazing my parents let me stay there at all. My mom knew I wasn't well, but she had no idea how bad it was.

I kept a shoebox under my bed to hold a mirror and razor blade. I couldn't live without the drug. I would lie awake at night and slide out the box time after time, lean over, and shove a rolled-up dollar bill up my nose to do a line, then stare at the ceiling praying for God or the devil to take my life. Just to fucking die. I had stopped looking at myself in the mirror and when I did I would pound my fists against it screaming "I fucking hate you!" and then just lean over time after time, blood draining from one of my nostrils onto the mirror. I didn't care—I dumped more blow out on the other side of the glass and tried to shove it up my other nostril, blocking out my pathetic life. Living itself had become a punishment and it was terror not to be high.

I began to pawn anything and everything I owned, starting with the jewelry Rick had given me. Then I would snort all that money away. I was stealing cash from my father's wallet when I ran out of funds late at night. Then I would pawn more jewelry and put the money back in my dad's wallet. Just so I wouldn't get kicked out. It was an insane cycle. But I needed a change of venue. I couldn't be loaded at my parents' house; I needed to find a private space.

By now I was buying small quantities of coke because I didn't have the cash anymore. Maybe $50 worth at a time. Scrounging the cash was hard. The high life was over, and when you're a drug addict, this time always comes. I had begun to circle the bottom. Gone were the days of fancy restaurants and dressing up; gone were the days of always having money or fancy cars. I was a drug addict. I was dying, and I was alone. Again.

My primary connection, a guy named Red, was always good to drop by and pick up without a call. He had a steady girlfriend and she never liked me when I came around. There was good reason for that. One particular Saturday afternoon I got lucky because Red's girlfriend was out, and that meant Red would turn me on to some blow and we would party for a while. We were sitting around doing lines and chit chatting (pretending to be social) all the while my mind was running on how to get more drugs from him. The fixation of cocaine had taken over and it was all I thought about. The obsession was deep in my veins. The set was simple: him happy I was there, me scheming how to separate him from his drugs.

Moments were simply fragments of time... He was telling me about his ex-wife and his girlfriend...he handed me a small silver spoon...little hits of blow each… Talking about his young son, and how his girlfriend went shopping, blah blah blah… More blow came out on the table. His life story… A few lines… How his girlfriend went out shopping for lingerie. More coke, he was now chopping lines up with a credit card, a huge pile in front of us. I was salivating, my senses fired… She wanted to bring another girlfriend in to have a threesome, and she was so high and she was wild and just strung out that it was impossible… He was talking but I didn't hear him… He poured out more coke. I was fixated… Fucking finally he handed me the straw… He continued with telling me she had a problem smoking base… Blah blah blah… BINGO… I hear smoking base…

"Oh, you're kidding? That's terrible, and you have children?"

More lines, more listening…more coke and how she was an awful person for his son.

"And she's around your small son? That's horrible."

By the time his girlfriend returned, Red told her to leave and never come back.

She went ballistic in the front yard. I heard a physical struggle and screaming. And just like that, she was replaced. By me. And the cocaine.

After two days of snorting, on one afternoon, Red gave me a bindle of blow with about four grams in it and a couple hundred dollars. I hadn't showered or changed my clothes in a few days. I had a bottle of perfume in the glove box of the truck I took from Rick. I just kept spraying it on my body. Showering was no longer a priority. With the money and the coke, I left. No explanation. After four hours, I returned. His friends were shocked. They thought I was like his last girlfriends. They had made money bets on me that I was gone as soon as I got drugs and money. I had filled up my gas tank and put oil in my car. The oil light had been on for a few weeks and I was afraid I would blow up my car. I had used all my money on drugs, not gas and oil. It had gotten to that. I could hear my father's voice in my head: "Always take care of your things, Dona," but none of those lessons mattered anymore. I was becoming feral. I had just gone to my parents' house and showered and picked up some clothes. Red took pride that I had just gone to clean up. I guess cleanliness separates a lot of people. He was happy I wasn't like the rest. The truth was, I would always go back to the source and I had enough drugs to get me back and forth.

Red seemed to have an endless supply hidden somewhere in the garage. I never asked where, because he was so generous. People came and went from the house. He was always going into the garage and coming out, then introducing me as his new girlfriend (even though I was still technically married to Rick), me making drinks and offering people lines. Such a lovely couple. We would sit up all night, night after night, doing lines, until, one night, out of nowhere, we decided to cook some up. We had been awake for a day or two and the time had come when snorting was no longer getting us high. Red had a different way of cooking the stuff up and he liked to make large quantities. He would immediately break off pieces and give them to me for later, pieces which I would hide like a chipmunk for when we would run out. As we settled in on his couch and fired up the glass pipe, that familiar high-pitched ear ringing hit like a freight train. Hard and fast. My heart beating, holding the thick, rich, hot smoke in my lungs as long as I could before the billowing of the exhale. And boom. Higher then I could ever be, reaching immediately for another hit.

By daylight Red told me he needed to sleep. He took some Valium and went to bed. I was paranoid, and the sun had come up. I could not remember where I had hidden the rock cocaine from the previous night and he had not cooked any more. I was slowly coming down and that old feeling of wanting to die was creeping in. Crawling on the carpet, desperate to find anything, I grabbed every little white speck and put it in the pipe and lit it, torching anything that would ignite. Sweaty and sticky, I began to come down and panic. I was crashing hard.

The fireplace walls were made of stone. I knew I had hidden rocks there, so I began to search. Climbing up the wall. I was completely spread out like Spiderman when Red walked out of the bedroom.

"What the fuck are you doing?"

I froze, eyes bulging out from my head, knowing he knew I was strung out. I told him about the lost rocks. He shook his head and walked by me to the kitchen. Sickened. As he ate breakfast he told me we had to stop. He was right. The run that had lasted a few days and I was going insane. He convinced me to get in the hot tub with him. Still with pipe in hand, I threw the glass pipes on the concrete patio and they shattered. I took some Valiums and crashed for a few days.

Coming too, I awoke and drove to my parents' house. Cosby had been calling my parents' home. He had been talking to my mom. She knew something was terribly wrong. He was concerned about me, she said. My weight was so low, and I would disappear for days at a time. She had mentioned how I left my husband because Cosby thought it was a good idea that we take a family vacation to Bill Harrah's ranch in Idaho. As I walked in, my mom was telling me the good news—which was the worst news I had ever heard. I couldn't imagine going anywhere without my drugs. Let alone to Idaho. I walked into my bedroom and stared at myself in the mirror. I slowly lifted my purple striped shirt up over my breasts. Looking at my own reflection was a sobering experience. I saw a little girl. She was emaciated. Her ribs were sticking out and she had no breasts. I saw her collarbones protruding and her wiry arms. Dark circles under the eyes of a skeletal face. I couldn't believe that was me. Standing there in my bedroom I had had since I was a child, with my rainbow wallpaper, looking in the mirror of my dresser I had had since I was a little girl, stood someone I didn't recognize.

"I'll go to Idaho if I can bring a friend," I told Cosby on the phone.

I didn't care that he assumed it was a girlfriend. I'd figure this out later. Fuck him, anyway.

Three days later I was on a private plane with my family landing in Idaho. In the back of the plane was Red trying to calm me down. He had just informed me he didn't bring any coke. My head was exploding. He had been thoroughly instructed (by me) to bring a minimum of an ounce.

Idaho was the most isolated place in the world. Not only was there nothing to do there, but also Red had brought his son. *Oh my fucking god. Are you kidding me.* It was hell the moment I stepped off the plane. Not only was I still feeling the effect of my last run—fatigue, depression, and agitation—but now this? I was like a hamster on a wheel. *Get me the hell out of here.* The cravings were still strong and the pipe was calling me. I didn't care that a river ran through there. I didn't care about a snake river and the people who worked there. I could barely stand Red sober. Okay, so I went horseback riding, and my mom loved this little boy. Who cared. I needed out of there. I wasn't hungry and I was aggravated the entire time. Nothing to do. Fuck. Horrible... It was a blur. I counted the days till I was out of there.

At 110 pounds, at Harrah's Ranch in Idaho.
A special invite from Cosby.

The moment the plane touched back down in Orange County, I told Red I would meet him at his house. He went to drop off his son. I stopped by the Raspberry Roach, a head shop in downtown Huntington Beach, to buy four glass pipes and a handful of butane torches. We were on. It was all I thought about in Idaho. My heart was racing; I couldn't drive fast enough. The guy at the counter knew what I was doing and was trying to invite himself along. I wanted nothing to do with him. In fact, I couldn't get out of there fast enough. The pipe was calling me.

When I arrived at Red's, he had already cooked up an enormous batch, enough for us to have our own pipes. We sat on the couch and took hit after hit, blowing our fucking minds out, doing lines in this low-ceilinged smoky room as well as drinking. He had rethought the notion that we needed to stop. He was just as addicted as I was. Finally.

Smoking all afternoon into the night, listening to the little pipes' crackling noises, we then moved into the hot tub out back, firing the pipe into the darkness, all talking ceased. There was nothing social about my behavior and I was beginning to get paranoid. My hearing awareness had increased, and every little sound became magnified by 1,000. I believed people were spying on us as I whispered to Red to look at the people by the fence.

He kept whispering, "There isn't anyone there," but I swore there were.

I began to see animals up in the trees and I could no longer be outside. The hallucinations had taken over. My world was slowly closing in. We went inside where my paranoia was only worse. I convinced Red there were people in the bushes in the front yard. Red pulled out two loaded handguns. I was now glued to the front window, stark naked, peeking out with one eye, careful not to let anyone see me. I had a pistol in one hand and a crack pipe in the other as I tried to explain to him the people were Vietcong with bamboo hats on their heads. They had guns and they were in the front trees as well. I stayed glued to the window all night.

The sun was just starting to go down on day three and we were drinking straight rum from the bottle now. I had to, to numb the pain of my bleeding tongue so I could continue to hit the pipe. MTV was blaring endlessly on his big screen TV. Duran Duran. Billy Idol. Fucking Haircut 100. There was a knock at the door, and we grabbed our guns and hid, fearing it was the police. It wasn't. There had not even been a knock. Everything was real, but nothing was real. Our world was a bleak, conniving house of mirrors.

Day after day, hit after hit, we cooked and smoked, my lips becoming dryer, my hair falling out. His son had been dropped off some time in those days and I slightly remember giving him a peanut butter and jelly sandwich at some point, thinking I was a good mother for feeding this child. Pouring him some orange juice. And then, as quickly as he appeared, he disappeared somewhere into my cloud. I never changed my clothes except to go into the hot tub. I was spraying on Ciara perfume thinking that it made me desirable. The hot tub had become my shower because I could smoke while I was in it. My tongue had cracked even more and started bleeding from the burn of the pipe and at some point I had become so paranoid I had moved into the dark bedroom. No lights, just the pipe and me. I was placing sheets and blankets over the windows. I had started to see flashing lights and I accused Rick of sneaking up and taking pictures of me. When that wasn't enough, I crawled into the closet, shutting the door behind me. It had been seven days of this insanity.

"Death," I prayed, "take me. Just fucking take me."

That's all I remember.

Fade to black.

I woke up in rehab. No idea how I got there. None whatsoever. Covered in bruises, ribs sticking out, my hips bones protruding and my hair falling out, I was a mess. On a day when all of my old girlfriends were graduating from Fountain Valley High School, getting their diplomas, moving tassels from right to left on their caps, signing yearbooks, planning farewell parties, and dreaming about college, I was near death in a rehab facility. There would not be any high school graduation for me. Not that day. Not ever.

For the next 60 days, pretty much the entire summer, I tried to get better. But it was hard. I started going to group therapy sessions to try and figure out what was wrong with me. I met lots of junkies and alcoholics. There were even famous athletes (though I recognized none of them). I knew that if I didn't get clean that I would die.

How had I gotten here? One moment I was a geeky, shy, awkward teenage girl, and then, almost overnight, I blossomed into someone that many used to refer to as "one of the prettiest girl in Orange County." Almost instantly I had a busy modeling and acting career and on the outside everything must've looked wonderful. But inside, I was still the same scared, awkward girl. I was dying inside. I was afraid that people would reject me if they knew the real me. The scared, insecure girl. I wasn't sure how to deal with all the attention I was getting. I became so busy being what everyone expected me to be because of how I looked that I couldn't cope (my mother always said I was built without a "coper" (that was, I didn't know how to cope).

And now I was all alone. Laying in my bed at rehab, there was one person I knew I could reach out to as I prepared to get released. Bill had been calling me while I was in there. I'd seen his name written on little pieces of paper taped up on the wall: messages he was leaving. Checking on me. That made me feel better. I'd been seeing him since I was 16, for more than two years, and obviously he still cared for me. I thought about all the trips we'd taken, the gifts he'd showered me with, and what he had done to help boost my career.

I needed to talk to him. He had always been there for me and always encouraged me to go to him for help, no matter what. It was what I needed; there was nobody else to turn to.

We talked. I told him, "I'm sober now. No more drinking. No more craziness. I'm clean. I'm changing my life. No wild behavior."

All I wanted was some new clothes, so I could feel pretty again. That's all I wanted. So I asked him if he would buy them for me.

"You know something?" he grumbled with an annoyed, dismissive edge. "You were a lot more fun before you got sober."

And that was the end of my teenaged relationship with Bill Cosby.

Dona Speir

Chapter Eleven
Back in the Game

DONA SPIER
MISS MARCH 1984

My Playboy promotional shot that went everywhere with me.

When I got out of rehab, I had no idea what I was going to do. I had no plans, I had no responsibilities, and, for the many people I had worked with in the past, I had all but ceased to exist.

The world had moved on even though it had only been 60 days. Being young, I was able to not only land on my feet but also recover physically at a fairly fast pace. I had gained my weight back and was, thankfully, looking like my previous photographs.

I wasn't really stressed out. For once it felt kind of nice to be out of the fast lane. There were no expectations or pressures being placed upon me and that felt good. But I also knew I was still very young and had a lot of life ahead of me. I needed to do something.

I decided to get back in touch with the agencies I had been working with. It had been a while and I wasn't sure how interested they would be, considering I had a slight accountability problem. I figured it might be worth a shot.

It was late August. Everyone was on hiatus. I had not worked in ages. Most print work was shut down. No one was filming anything.

I had gone back to David Wilder's office. He was my theatrical agent. I had had him for years. I'm not sure how I had originally engaged him, but he was your typical Hollywood cheeseball agent. He had way too many scantily dressed girls coming and going out of his office at all times. He wore a gold chain around his neck (it was the '80s). His shirt was usually unbuttoned one too many times as well. Always happy to see me, he had treated me differently once Bill had called him and told him how he was to manage me. Bill had lots of ideas about me and my career and he had no problem sharing them with David.

I remember telling him that I would take any role but I never wanted to speak.

He found that strange. He told me I was the only actress in LA that didn't want a speaking role.

Consequently, it seemed that every set I went on, even though I was hired not to speak, they always gave me lines and extra days of work. I was constantly reminding him I wasn't an actress.

David was responsible for getting me Taft Hartley'd into the union (which basically means getting me my union card). He booked me on an Aaron Spelling show. One of many in my career.

His office was right on Sunset Blvd. across from Le Dome restaurant. I had just gotten out of treatment and after all the running and gunning I was back at my parents' house living in my old room with my rainbow wallpaper yet again, another reminder that I just couldn't stand on my own two feet. Lying there many nights I wondered: how did I end up back here again?

That particular day was nothing special other that the streets seemed pretty empty and it was exceptionally smoggy.

I did not tell David I had been in rehab. Back then it was not trendy. In fact, I didn't know anyone who had been in rehab. He probably didn't even notice I was missing. I asked him what was going on in town. I had learned that when seeing an agent (of which I had many) to *always* tell them I was busy working elsewhere, therefore letting them think I was in demand.

He told me the big thing going on right now was Playboy's 30th anniversary girl search. It literally went in one ear and out the other. We continued to talk. We went to La Dome for lunch and then David brought it up again. I had never considered Playboy. First because of my father, who I know would have been shocked if I ever (publicly) posed nude, and second because I never considered myself Playboy material. I always thought those girls who did Playboy were more beautiful and more together than I was. Way more glamorous and special. Some sort of a secret club that I could never be good enough for, let alone some 30th anniversary thing.

They were big. I was little. They were special. I was not. I remember seeing the naked pictures Jack took of me. They looked nothing like the girls in Playboy. There would never be a chance the famed magazine would ever have me. That was the big time as far as I was concerned.

During lunch, David convinced me to walk two blocks down Sunset to the Playboy building. Just to talk. I had no idea what I would talk to them about. The entire thing seemed silly to me. He had called Marilyn Grobowski, the head editor for the magazine. He said he had a girl for them. I didn't know David would get a finder's fee for Playmates and a huge payoff for their 30th anniversary girl.

Walking into the main reception was incredibly intimidating. They had enormous (20-foot) centerfolds on their walls. Famous ones I remembered seeing. Marilyn greeted David and me and she took me back to the studio immediately.

It was an amazing experience. The sets were enormous for a still shoot. I think it was the first time I had seen an 8x10 Polaroid.

Everything happened in a blink of an eye. A whirlwind. I was going to talk and now I was having makeup put on? I was handed a robe and sent into a bathroom which was across from the makeup room. I came out and was immediately grabbed by a makeup woman named Tracy. She sat me down in this huge barber's chair and started talking to me. It was like a cartoon where you see people's mouths moving but you don't

Dona Speir

hear any noise. Someone had come in and asked me my shoe size. I think she had a southern accent and was telling me to relax. I couldn't understand why they were putting makeup on me for a quick Polaroid. At one point, she looked down at my hands on the arm of the chair and uncurled my fingers. They had been holding on so tight my knuckles had turned white.

She said there was nothing to worry about. After a quick patch job someone escorted me to a set. They had pulled the centerfold they were shooting off her set and gave me her "wardrobe." It consisted of a tiny red sweater. They showed me her picture and asked me to duplicate it. I slipped on the heels and took my place on her set and then they said "drop the robe." I froze. There were five to ten people running around. Adjusting lights, carrying things in the background. I heard voices behind the lights.

David had been removed and Marilyn's voice was there. "Drop your robe, please."

The room was huge with commercial height ceilings—everything echoed.

I was so uncomfortable. I had no idea how I had gotten here. How I woke up this morning and now I was in the Playboy building on a set. How all these people were waiting for me to stand here practically naked in front of them so they could look at me. Judge me. I was broken and damaged goods.

There were conversations I could not hear. Lots of whispering and pointing and furrowed brows. So many lights. Had I done something wrong? Was I wasting their time? What were they saying? The buzzing of activity grew more intense, and then I started to realize that they wouldn't be bringing more people out to see me unless they liked me. But how could this be? I wasn't Playboy material.

Was I?

Had I become so numb to my own self that I didn't even know what I looked like? Had my addiction rendered me incapable of even understanding who I was? Playboy models were voluptuous and beguiling and had mystique. They weren't like me. They lived glamorous and exotic lives. I was a recovering drug addict. I was an alcoholic. I had pushed life to the edge so many times it was a miracle I wasn't already in the ground.

I took a deep breath and dropped my robe and I waited. There was no reaction. Zero. The men in the back kept walking. People who were in mid-sentence continued talking, the camera assistants never really looked up at me. The only one in the room who was uncomfortable with my nudity was me. It finally hit me: they see naked girls all day long. Arny Freytag, the photographer, called out to me to look at this 8x10 Polaroid camera and to copy the pose. Easy enough. Just then, two people rushed out to me to touch my hair and to drape the tiny red sweater over my shoulders. It was such a big production. Nothing like I had experienced before. Not for a photo shoot. And as soon as it started, it was over. Just like that. Marilyn was happy, David was thrilled, and I was shuffled out the door.

It wasn't two days later I got a call from Playboy that they wanted to test me for a centerfold. They asked if I could come down and try on clothing for a shoot. I had not told my family and I wasn't about to yet. I drove to LA that day and they picked a wardrobe and prepared me for my test shoot the next day. The hunt for the 30th anniversary girl was coming to a close and I was a serious contender. They wasted no time. It was all happening so fast. One second I was being released from rehab and the next I was in front of a Playboy photographer in a huge Hollywood house they had rented for a photo shoot. Nearly in a blink of an eye.

Within two weeks I was okayed by Hef to shoot a centerfold. It didn't mean it would ever get published—it just meant that Playboy was willing to invest. Money. Shooting one was a process. Ten full days of work for one picture. Every day, sometimes mid-day having it checked by Hef to see if we were on the right track. Toward the end of the shoot I had to be sewn into my set standing on one leg, literally, the dress I was wearing was physically sewn into the backdrop to make it appear as if it was "floating." It was going to take literally ten days to shoot this one photo, *one single photo*. If that wasn't bad enough, the pose that they all agreed on did not show my pubic hair, and that was a problem, because they needed to see it. Being a natural blonde, I didn't have much hair to start with either. That was fine for the Japanese version since it is illegal in Japan to show pubic hair but it did not work for the American edition.

As soon as I got sewn into set, up on one foot in four-inch high heels, the makeup person would come and glue a toupee of sorts on my inner thigh. He had made it out of spirit gum and hair from my hairbrush. At night he would attach it to the makeup mirror not to lose it. It had become a comical act. This entire shoot. And they were wondering why they couldn't get a sexy expression from me. It was the only thing missing from my shoot. My part. I was tired by then. I was working seven to ten hour days plus driving sixty miles each way sometimes in traffic that could take up to two hours each way. I felt I just couldn't give them the right expression they were looking for. Not that I had a clue what they wanted.

After ten grueling days of shooting, I was approved. It still didn't mean I would be published. I had met some girls who shot a centerfold 12 months prior and had not been published and didn't have a date yet.

About this time, I was being introduced to the Playboy Mansion. My first visit was that summer. I was brought up to the mansion by Marilyn Grabowski. It was a Sunday evening. It was movie night. What an amazing place on a warm summer evening. I wore a white lace off-the-shoulder dress with a pink satin bow tied around my waist. Conservative but beautiful. The other girls were scantily dressed, but I wasn't raised that way. When I was introduced to Hef, he made a comment about my pictures and how much he liked them and also that he liked my conservative dress. He smiled when he walked away. I don't remember much of the night. Just the warm summer breeze and the beauty of the backyard.

The news broke that I didn't make 30th anniversary girl. It was late September. The good news was that I was given a month. March. I was going to be Miss March. I was disappointed because of the financial aspect, but being given a month was an honor. There were still many girls waiting for the news I received. In fact, the gal who was pulled off her set for me to take a Polaroid still had not been given a month.

Chapter Twelve
Becoming a Playmate

Early on, me signing by myself at an Auto-Rama show.

Going to rehab was the farthest thing from my mind. I had already spent two days testing to decide if Playboy was going to invest in a centerfold shoot for me.

Once Hef gave the clearance, the next move was scheduling a date for the centerfold itself.

It was a ten-day shoot. Every night Hef received film and 8x10 Polaroids to okay or tweak. What we originally started with and what was published was an entirely different centerfold. I remember hearing the Police song "Every Breathe You Take" playing on the radio in the background, over and over and over. I always felt it was God telling me He was watching over me. I had begun to get some sort of spiritual life in rehab and I had taken it with me and was practicing it.

Once the centerfold decision was made, the next thing to do was shoot what was called "small camera" or 35 mm. Most woman shot at

Dona Speir

their hometown or on set in LA. They never really looked at me as a glamorous girl. I was always a beach girl. Very little makeup and hair. Always that rolled-out-of-bed-into-the-sand look.

They originally shot my small camera images in San Luis Obispo on a nude beach. I guess they thought they could get better shots. For some bizarre reason, for one of the first times Playboy made a special request to shoot out of the country. We were the guests of Fonature, Mexico's company for tourism. I'm not sure if it was an idea from Cancun Mexico or Playboy but I was the girl that got us out of the country.

We all got ready to go and off we went for two weeks. I had no idea where Cancun was or what to expect. I wasn't very well traveled outside of the United States. Cancun at that time only had four or five major hotels and hadn't been developed. All of Playa del Carmen was a jungle.

We stayed at the Fiesta Americana and I had the Presidential Suite to myself. The crew kept all the camera gear in one of the bedrooms. One day, after a particularly hard day shooting barefoot, I went into the camera room. The air conditioner worked best there. I was talking on the phone and I discovered if I took their air can and turned it upside down the compressed air was super cold. I sat on the phone and sprayed cold air on my sore feet until there was none left. Two days later, my photographer, Arny Freytag, dropped his Polaroid camera in the sand. When they went for the compressed air, it was gone. All six cans. I had to fess up.

I was up every morning at 3:00–4:00 a.m. to get camera ready then drive to some location. Chitzen Itza, Playa del Carmen, Tulum, somewhere close to the border of Belize. We were coming home late at night long after the sun went down. Then there were always the late dinners with Fonature.

We went climbing on ancient pyramids. We dodged stingrays in the water and wild monkeys by the beach. We met with owners of Club Med and were constantly on the go.

There was a time our van went down on a jungle road and we literally caught a ride in the back of a truck filled with tires in the middle of the jungle. It was about two hours from our hotel. Huge bugs were hitting me from every angle. There we were, all of us balancing on used tires.

Then there was the day we were shooting on the beach and forgot the cooler of food. All we had was our cooler of Coca-Cola. Our driver, who spoke no English, climbed a tree for coconuts and we traded Coca-Colas for tortillas from a woman making them in her hut with a dirt floor and peacocks running in and out. Arny took a Polaroid of their family. They had never had a picture taken of them. The little girl collected conch shells and tried to sell them on the highway. The conch shell and the little girl made their way into my Playboy issue. I keep the conch shell in my office.

Looking back, it was a lot of work but a lot of fun. We had many social engagements, being there as guests of the state, Quintana Roo. Being 19 and on a beach photo shoot, I did not bring fancy clothes, so the night we had dinner with the governor at his mansion threw me off guard. Our stylist did her best, but most of the garments she brought were very small articles of clothing. She had gone down to a little store in town (what there was of a town then) and purchased some sort of lingerie thing and made a dress for me.

Needless to say, all the women who were at the governor's party knew I was in pajamas. It was not only embarrassing, but uncomfortable. Being awkward in these setting was the new norm for me. The voice of Cosby playing in my ear saying "You don't know how to dress," or the photographer saying "You can't do your own damn makeup," or Rick saying "You can take the girl out of the gutter, but you can't take the gutter out of the girl" all formed a critical chorus in my head that was distracting. It was just like when I was younger. My skin just a little too tight. Always feeling like I was on the outside of the conversation. Feeling like they forgot to give me the playbook to life. Wearing pajamas to the governor's house. My mother was right: I couldn't do anything right.

The day eventually came when I took my first drink. Again.

They had warned me in rehab that would happen—that I would start to drink again. I knew the drugs would kill me over time. The overdoses, the incredibly bad people, the scary places I had been trapped within. The dark memories were still vivid but my body had recovered. Alcohol had never brought me there. In fact, alcohol was still somewhat mysterious. It was a social thing, right? In the end of my cycle before rehab, I chose drugs over alcohol. I never believed alcohol was my problem.

It is amazing how deep denial runs for an alcoholic/addict.

The truth was, I wasn't even old enough to take a legal drink in either Mexico or the US. I had forgotten about the trouble alcohol had brought about. I had forgotten about all the lies I'd told regarding alcohol. I had forgotten about the night I had a stranger drive me home from a concert at the LA Forum because I got separated from my group and lost both my shoes, never making it inside. I had forgotten about the first time I drank as a kid. That I violently threw up, cried, and that my brother had to pick me up and carry me into my bedroom. What I did tell myself was, I had never gotten a DUI, nor spent time in jail. I had no severe consequences from alcohol. At that point in my life it was just a gateway drug, used only to come down off harsher chemicals or in addition to more chemicals. Yes, chemicals were my problem. Drugs were my problem. Cocaine was my problem.

The day I picked up a drink, I had no intention of drinking. I was no longer practicing a 12-step program, and getting back in the game of life was more important than spiritual principals anyway. I had lost almost a year of sobriety to misuse of pills over my wisdom teeth coming out. That was about a year after I went through rehab at 18 years old. My pride did not allow me to start over and I was gone like a bird.

That morning we woke up and shot photos of me around the hotel. It was fabulous. Afterwards, we had the late morning off and were to resume shooting in the early afternoon.

I was told not to get my hair wet and to avoid destroying my makeup under any condition. That was always a given, considering it took hours to look like I just got out of bed and wasn't wearing any makeup. Ironic.

In the early afternoon, I had a teenage brainstorm. I was having none of their rules. While they were enjoying a late lunch in an oversized *palapa*, I decided to go waterskiing. I hired a boat and skied right past the crew. I remember waving as I flew by. "Hey, guys!"

Needless to say, they were not amused; in fact, the makeup artist was pissed. After returning to the beach, I headed for my room. I showered and then went through the entire process again, this time with a whining makeup artist lecturing me for an hour or more about how irresponsible and selfish I was.

"Do you have any idea how much money your behavior costs?"

I had not had a day off in ten days (neither had they). I was punchy. I didn't care. I would ask for forgiveness, not permission. The selfishness had already begun.

After our shoot during the "golden hour," which is late in the day when the light is perfect, the crew took over the bar. I usually didn't join them. But this time, when the cocktail waitress came around and asked for orders, I spoke up. "I'll have something."

Arny looked at me, surprised. "Dona, I thought you don't drink?"

"I think I will tonight," I said.

It had been so long since I drank that I barely even knew what to order. I paused, holding everyone's order up. I ordered a White Russian. It was the only thing I could think of. I remember thinking about what they said in rehab, how they said I would die if I drank again. "To drink was to die." I always pictured a person immediately keeling over and dying with a drink in his hand. I drank. Lo and behold, nothing happened. Absolutely nothing. It was sweet and warm and delicious. I immediately ordered a second, then went to order a third, when Arnie Freytag cut me off.

"No, Dona. Enough. We have an early call tomorrow."

I walked back to my room that night, smiling to myself as I walked, surprised I had a slight stagger after just two drinks. My tolerance had clearly gone down, but the booze was an old friend. It owned a part of me.

I managed to get through the rest of the shoot without causing too much trouble. I drank a couple more times, but kept things under control. It wasn't like I was diving back in headfirst. I was only dipping my toes into the pool to test the water. Still, deep down I knew I shouldn't have made the impulsive decision to start drinking again.

We were down there for a few more days and then it was over. I had no idea what the pictures would look like. I was so self-critical that I imagined them getting back to Los Angeles and saying, "We've made a mistake. There's no way she is Playboy material." I was such a damaged and insecure girl. But I looked a certain way and that's how I was now being judged. By my beauty. On the flight back home to California, as I stared out the window, it was hard not to think about how my modeling career had started. I thought, *nothing can justify the damage that Jack did to me.* The fact that I was going to have my own Playboy issue was exciting in a weird way. But honestly, I still wanted to be a florist. I was still upset that my life had become so compromised at such an early age. But there was no changing my reality; I could only wait and see how everything looked in the magazine. What would the reaction be? What would people say about me? What would this do to my life?

Chapter Thirteen
My Issue

Fame comes in all shapes and sizes. If you appear in a movie or television show, people might start recognizing you. Same thing goes for commercials. But nothing really prepared me for what it would be like when you had your own issue of Playboy. I remember when I saw my issue for the first time. It actually was kind of anticlimactic. It was mid-January and my issue wasn't due out on the stands for another two weeks. I had been drinking in a little bar in SoHo on Prince Street in New York City. I had a New York agent by then and was doing shooting for Cosmopolitan and some other editorial work. But there I was, walking back from a bar, and peeking out at me through the window of a small Korean market was the March 1984 issue. I had not seen it yet. Funny how Playboy doesn't give the Playmates a copy before it hit the stands. A little electrical shock went through my body. It became very real. It was in print. There was no turning back now. What pictures had they chosen?

I bought four copies that night. My coat was tightened up to my neck. Being from California, I didn't own a scarf, and that January night I was freezing as I huddled under the street lights trying to read the words they had written. "Girl on The Run" they had titled the article. *How appropriate*, was my first thought. Then I saw the pictures. Some good, some great, then some I swore I didn't take. How in the hell did they get that angle?

When my plane touched down at LAX a few days later, my mom and dad were both there to pick me up. We had worked out a fragile peace by then once I had gotten out of rehab and had started really working again. There were two pictures in my layout I wasn't particularly fond of, both with my legs apart. For one pose I had tried to copy a shot by the playmate Ruth Guerri. She was another centerfold, and I liked how she had had her knees together, but they caught me in mid-shot, thus blowing the effect. The other was a hammock shot where I was nude and putting my foot down to stop the hammock from swinging. Either way, there I was: all of me.

From my place in the back seat of the car, like I was 12 again, I handed the magazine to my mother, and swallowed hard. They had not seen me naked since I was probably 4 or 5 years old. She too tried to read the issue in the dark by the lights on the side of the freeway. To my surprise, they both seemed really interested, intrigued, and even excited by what they saw and read. Had I finally achieved something in their eyes?

By the time my issue hit the stands, the craziest of all things started to happen. First of all, Playboy magazines were now something laid out on our family coffee table. Previously they were something hidden under my dad's side of the mattress. Next, complete strangers, as in friends of neighbors, started knocking on our door. I would come home and my mom would be talking to people who were there waiting to get a magazine signed. Or there were stacks of magazines dropped off at the door with the same requests. But the oddest of all was when my father started to bring home my edition. His friends at the office had been requesting personally signed copies. We would talk at the dinner table about how people came up to him at work and congratulated him. It was a completely foreign concept to me. He seemed sheepishly impressed.

Fan mail continue to pile up at home and my mom helped me sort through it all. I was getting literally hundreds of letters every day and we were encouraged by Playboy to answer as many as we could. Always including autographed pictures. I'll never forget one that really jumped out at me. It was from a shy bartender who worked at a restaurant called Gladstone's in Malibu. He was also a college student. He wrote me saying his roommate thought he was crazy for reaching out to me because there's no way I would ever respond. There was something very sweet and earnest about this letter. Explaining he had never in his life written a piece of fan mail. A few days later we had our monthly meeting up with Playmate Promotions. A few Playmates were talking about what to do after the meeting and I mentioned the sweet young bartender. They all agreed he needed a visit. I grabbed the girl who was on the cover of my issue and two other playmates and the four of us actually headed down to the restaurant where he worked, Gladstone's on Pacific Coast Highway near Malibu. We found him behind the bar, and all went over to him to autograph our respective issues and give him a kiss on the cheek.

I smiled at him and said, "Now you've got a story for your roommate. You can tell him just how wrong he was."

I liked moments like that when we were able to make somebody's day just by paying a little attention to them.

In our matching costumes once again on the road.
(Me center back).

Playmate Promotions then put me on the road. I was to travel with other Playmates of the month to sign autographs and do personal appearances. My first stop was in Cleveland, Ohio; one of many towns that was a complete blur. By Cleveland, I was already drinking regularly again. This first trip was difficult but interesting—a huge learning curve for me. I was definitely green. The best part was visiting a veterans' hospital. The worst part was how tight all the other Playmates seemed to be. They had been together for some time and breaking in with them was tough. I was an outsider. Maybe that's why I started drinking a bit more than I should have on the road.

Dona Speir

Chapter Fourteen
Facing the Devil

When my issue of Playboy came out, my world was changed quickly. It was a big deal. But in the back of my head, there was something that seriously needed to be fixed. That same dark secret I couldn't push away.

Playboy had a letters column in the front of the magazine. It was a place where readers could write in and talk about prior playmates or send pictures that they had taken of them while they were first beginning their modeling career. I was always aware of that column and I think that's what triggered my brain to take action. I started thinking back to being upstairs at Jack's house in Fountain Valley. I think I was just starting to accept that that he had been grooming me. He was not a "real" photographer. He set that whole studio up in his house with a makeup room and a costume room as a front to lure in vulnerable young girls. At this point, that was totally obvious. But I started thinking back to the nude photos he had shot of me. The photos where he dressed me up in costumes that would humiliate me. I started to think, *what if he goes to Playboy or someplace else and tries to capitalize on those images?* What did occur to me was that he would want to show everyone that he shot me naked first. That he was something special and that *he* should be published. That he had some weird ownership of me. After the way he wouldn't let me go and the way he raged when I finally got away, I put nothing past him.

I was so frightened. Was my new career going to end before it even really started? He was the monster that never stopped haunting my dreams. Being so young, I still turned everything into "my fault." Every touch that man laid upon me was my fault. The worst was that every dollar of my father's hard earned money that he took was my fault. Every naked 15-year-old picture he had taken of me was my fault. Not because I had wanted to but because I was manipulated into doing it. Brainwashed and intimidated. I was so ashamed and had tried so desperately to get away from him. And when I couldn't, that was my fault too.

And I was angry.

I was just starting to come to grips with what he had done to me. The more I thought about it, the more of a criminal he seemed to be. How many other girls had he set up in that small studio? I would never find out, of course, but my hunch was that it was many. I felt emboldened. I was tired of having him in my thoughts, this threatening figure that had abused me. I was going to confront him once and for all and have him destroy every single negative he had of me.

I was mad. In fact, I was fucking irate and he was going to know it. He was going to know that he would never ever come near me again. Looking back on it, I almost can't believe I really did this. I was still very scared when I thought about him and what he did to me, but I was also growing up, and I was ready to begin confronting the people who had hurt me.

I drove over to the house on Hemlock Circle. I parked in the cul-de-sac and knocked on his door. He was surprised to see me, yet very happy. His smiled told me how he had taken credit for my accomplishments. I followed him up to his sickening studio, which seemed so much smaller now. He started to speak but I was having none of it.

"I want every single negative you have of me destroyed," I demanded. I didn't waste any time.

He seemed startled and a bit confused. "Are you kidding?" He started to shuffle and was pleading with me not to do this.

I was not kidding. It was late afternoon and I could smell the familiar gin and tonic coming from his breath.

"No," I told him. "I'm dead serious."

My anger had overridden my fear. Once in the darkroom where I knew he kept all of his negatives, prints, and contact sheets, I watched him carefully as he produced every single one. And I made sure that he did in fact pull out all of them, including the pictures of me on the walls.

I stood there and watched him use the paper cutter on them, each and every one, while, over and over, he kept saying, as if to himself, "These are such beautiful images. Are you sure?" Trying to talk me out of it. All the while telling me about the new nudes of new girls he was currently shooting. Girls running pearls between their legs and other sexual oddities. Offering to show me the shoots. My stomach was beginning to churn with that familiar sickening feeling, but I stuck to my guns and didn't move from the table. I got my way.

As I watched my pictures and negatives shred in front of me, I felt a little bit lighter. Looking back, it was the first time I felt tall in his studio. When I saw the nude images get destroyed, he finally lost his power over me. I would have a lot of things left to worry about in my life, but this was not going to be one of them. Because I was so young and naïve, it never occurred to me that I was a minor when he took those. He could have gone to jail if that fact was discovered. But I didn't understand that his actions were illegal. Touching me was a crime he should have paid for. Instead, I was the one who would pay for his actions for many years.

Dona Speir

Chapter Fifteen
Almost Famous

In the early '80s, Playboy centerfolds were truly rock stars, or so we thought. When companies booked us to come make an appearance, we would roll into town and take names. Whether it was a beer company or some sporting event or whatever, every red carpet would be rolled out and we would paint the town in colors it had never seen before.

We would go on the radio to promote our appearances in that particular city and then all hell would break loose. Whether it was ten or fifty of us, thousands of guys would always show up to ask for autographs, buy us drinks, and, of course, try to get in our pants.

The crowds we walked out to every night at Auto-Ramas.
It was insane. They never let up.

Looking back on those days, I'm not sure how our den mothers dealt with all of it. Valerie Cragin was the head of Playmate Promotions at the time and it was her job to herd the wildest bunch of girls, day in and day out. I honestly don't know how she did it. Or even why. I remember her as a chain-smoking woman with a semi-beehive hairdo. She would call everyone "dawling" and was a den mother left over from the '60s. Valerie Cragin and I got along well. She had written a book called Method Modeling and I'm surprised she didn't make us walk with a book on our heads. She was extremely strict with us girls. She held the key to what money we would make doing appearances so we had to go along with her outdated shenanigans. She made sure we all had our "playmate self-defense classes" and matching silly outfits.

Early on, we did the "AutoRama" car show circuit. It was a huge indoor muscle car convention show that traveled around city to city in the winter. Mostly Midwest. It was actually an enormous attraction with a circus-style vibe. We would get there on a Thursday (which we always complained about), then do our radio shows and the local live Good Morning shows starting Friday morning. Friday at lunch the sponsoring radio would run contests to have lunch with a Playmate. It was an enormous event. The poor guys had no idea what they were walking into. It wasn't a table set for two. It was usually two enormous banquet tables with the men sitting on one side and us girls seated on the other as security. In the middle of us girls were the sponsors of the event, as well as the radio hosts and various other people. Playboy would never allow us to be auctioned off. Or so Valerie said.

But in every city at these car shows, all of this took place, and, mostly, the guys talked amongst themselves and they brought our issues to be signed. It never really had anything to do with them. It was all promotional. I never really minded it; I was always happy to be working. At night we would walk out to crowds that had been waiting for hours to get our autographs. We were paid $300 a day, working up to 11 hours a day with a break in the evening before going on stage. We were not paid travel days and AutoRama insisted we fly in the day before and fly out the day after, swearing that they could get sued if we didn't show up at advertised times. I always knew this was nonsense.

When we weren't on stage signing autographs or doing promotions for the event, we girls were just hanging out. It was always the winter months so we had to be creative. Going out at night, other than the hotel, was pretty much out of the question. We worked nights and it was always freezing. Plus, Valerie was always on our collective tails. On

Saturdays, a lot of times we would pile into each other's rooms and order pizza or go ice skating. We were always in the downtown area of wherever we were staying and there wasn't a lot to do, just mostly talk on the phone and order room service. We weren't really allowed to go anywhere. At least not far. I wasn't used to such cold temperatures and I remember freezing my first year on the road. The shows became a blur but they were steady income between modeling gigs and TV spots.

The first few car shows I went on were larger. I was baffled at the fact that hundreds and hundreds of boys and men would line up for hours before we got on stage. Just waiting for us. It seemed ridiculous to me.

The car show circuit always had a sprinkling of soap opera stars or B television stars on their own stage. Occasionally they mingled with us girls and were always positioned on the other end of the show. The "stars" got preferential treatment. They were paid to appear, paid per autograph, flown in on Friday, flown out on Sunday. I always argued with Valerie about our worth. That we should be demanding more money. If she was willing to give us away, then they would take it, I stressed to her (to no avail). I recall in one city having shared some time with Alan Thicke and dancing the peppermint twist with him on stage while Chubby Checker sang. You really never knew what you were going to get from city to city. Always something there for every age, and, for me, partying like a Playmate was becoming a typical occurrence.

Alan Thicke and I after doing the Peppermint Twist together.

Over the years, Playmate Promotions slowly changed with the times. Playboy was being accepted into the Bible Belt and advertisers like Proctor & Gamble were lightening up with the Playboy image. Thank goodness, because I remember losing a hair commercial once P&G found out I was a centerfold! Playboy had its own singing Playmates, different Playmate ball teams, and I was part of the Playboy Broadcasting team. The Playboy brand was growing fast and there was something for everyone.

At one point I traveled to Argentina to open up the Argentinean issue of Playboy. It was an enormous opportunity. I was chosen because I was a solid worker who had good work ethics and was dependable. Kudos to my dad for instilling lessons that still managed to rear their heads once in a while. Playboy knew they could trust me to represent them well. I was to be that country's first centerfold as well as their cover girl, only to find out once I got to Buenos Aries that I would be their second centerfold. That did not sit well with me from the beginning. It was always something with them. I had done all their press tours, magazine ads, and television from the moment I touched down in Buenos Aries. I had been replaced by a Miss Argentina for centerfold. The night of the opening gala I was supposed to jump out of a front-facing life-size box with the rabbit logo. They had made the front of the box with some sort of synthetic material. They were afraid I wouldn't be able to get out. They were right. How many Playmates does it take to get out of a box? Well, just one, if you don't mind blood.

My Playboy cover in Argentina.

They put me into the box with no lights and handed me a razor. They told me when the time came and I got my cue, to cut my way out. It was completely dark when they placed me in. What they didn't tell me was that it was a dual-edged straight razor. When I went to cut my way out, I sliced my fingers and hand open and became a bleeding centerfold. To numb the pain and embarrassment, I began downing cocktail after cocktail that night. Eventually someone offered me cocaine, and I snatched it up. Even though I had promised myself I would never do that drug again after going through rehab, I didn't care. The entire trip was such a disaster as far as I was concerned. I just wanted to blot it out.

The rest of the night was a blur. 500 people came to see me and Miss Argentina carried the ball. I was a drunken mess in a ball gown. Still, I was able to shift the blame like any good alcoholic or addict. The truth was I was angry and disappointed in them.

With Carl Lorimar, far right, drunk at the Midsummer Night's Dream Party.

On the set of Dragnet with Dan Aykroyd and Tom Mankewicz.

During my drinking days, unable to remember what I was shooting, with David Lee Roth.

My mom and dad at the unveiling of my centerfold on the wall at the Playboy Club.

With Andy and Arlene Sidaris and Joe Bob Briggs in NYC for the premiere of "Hard Hunted."

The unveiling of my centerfold at The Playboy club in Century City.

Drunk at the Playboy Mansion with Hope
Carlton and Dudley Moore.

Signing autographs with Pat Morita
for our film "Do or Die."

Drew Carey and I at Playboy Mansion
party. I never knew who I would meet.

Signing Autographs with Erik
Estrada in Las Vegas for our film
"Guns."

Hef and I
at a Playmate of the Year luncheon.

With comedian Pauly Shore
at a personal appearance.

On set with Hope Marie Carlton in
Hawaii for "Savage Beach."

Back in the game—
a Billboard in Manhattan.

On the road for Playboy signings with
eight of us gals. This was a crazy trip.

With Roberta Vasquez filming
"Guns."

On the set of the show "Columbo."

Dona Speir

The picture given to Cosby
and the first *real* photograph
taken of me by a professional
photographer. 16 years old. He
wanted to meet me after this.

ZED Cards, how a model is promoted
and advertised.

Sports and Fitness,
German Edition.

Playboy cover, Japanese edition.

My New York Zed Card.

Dona Speir

Me at The Lynn House today.

My father and I.

At my high school graduation
with my son.

My son Grayson and I.
It's just who we are.

The beginning of my modeling career.

My son and I. Millions of dollars could never replace what we share.

My co-writer and dear friend Chris Epting

Dona Speir

Chapter Sixteen
Hef

I always respected Hef, but I also feared him. I mean, ultimately he was the boss. I had heard too many stories up at the mansion about girls who had fallen into his web and were unable to come out unscarred. It's like any business. When you start having personal relationships during company time, very little good usually comes from that. It was no different at the Playboy mansion, just on a much, much weirder scale.

One of my biggest concerns at the mansion was Hefner's girlfriend at the time, Carrie Leigh. She was one of the most beautiful women I had ever seen. Absolutely striking. I had nothing against her personally. She seemed fine. I mean as fine as one of Hef's girls gets. The issue was she was bisexual. Again, I have absolutely no problem with that. But I had heard stories about Carrie seducing other girls at the mansion, and let's just say it never really worked out well for them in the end. That's why, whenever I visited the mansion, whenever I saw her, I would simply blast out a quick "Hi there!" and move on as quickly as I could without any sort of meaningful engagement. That was simply a trap I never wanted to fall prey to.

For the most part, I managed to avoid any kind of situation that might have resulted in something I did not want to do. But there's always that one day where things are just a little bit beyond your control.

One day, I arrived at the mansion and Carrie saw me coming.

"Come on!" she said excitedly. "Let's go shopping!"

I don't think it was me in particular—it could have been anyone. She just wanted out of the mansion and I was there in between interviews.

She summoned the limousine that was always at her disposal and we were whisked off into Beverly Hills and along Melrose and the number of other shopping districts not too far from the sanctuary of the mansion. She shopped her brains out and I, for the most part, played along. We actually had a fun day. But when I sensed her getting a little too close, I carefully maneuvered and made sure we had the distance I needed to protect myself. As soon as we got back to the mansion after our shopping spree, I quickly bid goodbye and headed to the guesthouse where I locked myself down for a few hours and stayed out of sight and out of trouble until traffic passed.

The "no rules" rules were always strange at the mansion. I was welcome to come and go as I pleased. I spent many days sunbathing by the pool alone or with other girls. Occasionally an Emu would come up from behind and peck at my chair. But the rules were the strangest.

See, Hef was nocturnal. He slept most of the day and would arrive down the stairs in the late afternoon/early evening. He had a personal assistant named Joni that us girls called "the Gargoyle of the Mansion." She was an older, scary (to me at least) pale brunette that had some strange relationship with him. She might have been an old centerfold, and there was always chitter chatter that her son might have been Hef's.

So, during the day, while all the Playmates were out on cattle calls for jobs, we would stop by for lunch and gossip. If we were still there before Hef came downstairs from his bedroom, Joni's job was to shoo us out of the main house. She did it by evil looks and weird language. Never direct, just weird. The mansion was always a semi-frightening place for me. During my first year as a Playmate, it was important for me to subtly make my case for being Playmate of the Year. Those were the exact words I was told by Marilyn Grawbowski. I wasn't sure how to do that. It was a delicate tightrope walk. Trying to be friendly to Hef without getting too close, fearing a proposition to sleep with him or Carrie. Trying to be visible enough to keep working for Playmate Promotions, dodging Carrie Leigh's advances (she flirted with me whenever she saw me), showing up for movie night Friday and Sunday nights, staying visible but being invisible to the wrath of Jonie. Being at the Playboy Mansion was like walking through a minefield.

Hugh Hefner and Playboy owned 50% me. It always felt like there was a carrot dangling in front of my nose. Within reach, possibly if I gave in sexually, but not guaranteed. The rules changed with every girl every day. My safety nets were two things: living 60 miles away from Los Angeles and having three other talent agencies I could make a living from, though Playboy was my primary bread and butter at the time.

Playboy's unspoken message was this: "Dona, you are wanted; you're just wanted the way we want you: by yourself, half naked, and available whenever we need you. Then, if we see fit, we will put more pictures of you in the magazine."

Looking back, it was incredibly heavy-handed, and even a little weird, right down to the way they paid us. We received $5,000 when we were done shooting, $5,000 when the magazine came out, and the last $5,000 a year after publishing date. They told us it was for our own good, for "tax reasons," but who really knows. Because I was so young, I never questioned it. In fact, I never questioned anything because I was so scared. The truth is I was angry that I needed Playboy more than they ever needed me. And that's how they get you.

Dona Speir

Chapter Seventeen
Goofy Guys

One of the funny and more interesting aspects of being a Playmate centerfold is how both famous and semi-famous men begin to seek you out. They don't know you, they don't know anything about you but they see your photo and they just decide they want you.

I have many stories, so many in fact they could probably fill their own book. I don't want to bore you, and trust me a lot of the stories really are boring, but I thought I would share a couple of moments that still ring funny for me.

Remember "Jethro" from the Beverly Hillbillies? That's Max Baer Jr. He went from being an actor to a director, and, not long after my issue came out, he began contacting me. Somehow he got my phone number. The phone number to my parents' home, that is. He called and called and called. Made great friends with my mom. I just kept telling my mom I would call him back. He persisted for months. At the nagging of my mother, I told her I would go on a date with him.

But instead of a traditional "take me out to dinner" date, I invited him to my parents' house for dinner. I figured that would get rid of him. I lived about 50 miles out of Beverly Hills and no one in their right mind would drive to the parents' house of a girl for dinner. Right?

Well, I had him figured wrong. Max had no problem with that. He showed up one night, a big bear of a guy, lots of gold chains and attitude, and he joined us at our table for dinner. And it was actually as normal as it could've been. My parents thought he was funny and interesting, and, honestly, he was. But boy, was he loud. He seemed smart and had a lot of experience in the industry, I just wasn't interested in him as a boyfriend, or anything else, for that matter. He was too old and too persistent and too pushy for me. He offered me everything. And I mean everything. I went to his home to visit one day. When I came out of the house, he had an enormous box with a red bow and an even bigger stuffed bear in the front seat of my car ("Baer"/"bear," get it?) Inside the enormous box was a red fox coat. I did not want to keep it. That was never my style. I shut the box without trying it on and pushed it back at him. It was too late. Max had had it inscribed "To Dona, Love Max" from Beverly Hills Furriers (I still keep it in the same box today).

Another one of these moments was when baseball star Reggie Jackson decided that he wanted to date me. This was around the same time as Max. My life was really becoming a blur. It's not that I didn't have respect for Reggie—I simply had no idea who he was. I had met him at an autograph signing. He was at one end of the Anaheim convention center and I was at another. He had asked for my number regarding what seemed like work or something. I was traveling for Playmate Promotions and I had just moved into a little house with my best friend Kristi. Kristi and I were constantly burning the candles at both ends. She helped hold the fort down while I was on the road, answering the phone and taking messages from my agents and helping me do so many things. She also was the funniest girl I've ever known, constantly playing tricks on me while I was away. I'd come home in the middle of the night from a trip and she would have rearranged the furniture. I'd take two steps into the house and I'd drop my keys. They would hit the floor. I'd hear a laugh from the bedroom. The table that was supposed to be by the door was no longer there. I'd take four steps in and hit my shin. I'd hear another full-blown guffaw from the bedroom and Kristi would be in a ball laughing while I'd be swearing. She would have moved another table so I'd bruised my shin. This is the house where I gave Kristi the nickname "Trixie" for all of the tricks she played on me in the '80s.

Reggie Jackson was one of the phone callers Kristi had been fielding for months. She just didn't know what to do with him. He had been asking her to have me call him back and I said I would but I didn't. One afternoon I was driving home from Los Angeles. I had a late afternoon flight and I called Kristi to let her know I was on my way home. Car phones had just been installed in cars and I could hear in her voice she was up to something. She was so excited to hear from me and asked what time I would be home exactly. I told her about one hour. I knew there was something up. In 15 minutes I called her back. She answered the phone on the first ring. I could hear more excitement…just like a 5-year-old child.

"What's up, Dona?"

"What's up, Kris?"

"Nothing, just glad you're back in town," she said, giggling

I hung up the phone. Sitting in traffic, I definitely knew she was up to no good. The last time I came home she had wallpapered the house. Not just the bedroom walls like we agreed with the landlord. She had wallpapered any and everything. The refrigerator, the bathroom scale, the window slates in the bathroom, my desk drawers, my pencil holder—basically anything she felt like. It was apparent Kristi needed adult supervision. It had been almost 45 minutes since my initial call. I called Kristi again.

This time she couldn't hold back. "I invited Reggie Jackson over. He'll be here when you get home," she said, practically rolling on the floor.

I hung up. I pulled the car off the freeway. I called Kristi back for the fifth time. "I'm not coming home. Jokes on you."

"You can't do this. What am I going to do with him?"

"I don't know, you invited him, you figure it out," I said, trying not to cry with laughter.

Reggie Jackson did come over to our li'l wallpapered house. She completely expected me to come home. When I didn't, she gave him a screwdriver and had him fix anything that was loose. He also repaired a few other things that didn't need fixing. When he finally escaped, his car alarm went off and he got stuck. He couldn't get his car started. I guess it went off for a half an hour.

Neither Kristi nor I ever heard from Reggie again.

I didn't see Reggie again until years later. I ran into him in line in a coffee house. He told me how crazy he was about me back then. I thanked him for fixing everything in our li'l wallpapered house. Well, that didn't stop the baseball superstar. You should know, I know very little about baseball and I could really care less about how famous somebody is. That's never made much of an impression on me. But to

Dona Speir

millions, Reggie Jackson is a hero and I'm sure he's used to much better treatment than I gave him.

My best friend Kristi and I.

Chapter Eighteen
Meeting "Hitler"

Another year or so after my issue of Playboy issue came out, I was now living in a rent-controlled apartment in Santa Monica to be closer to work opportunities in Los Angeles. Once again that looming feeling of hopelessness had begun to creep in. Even with all the new buzz and excitement that Playboy had whirling around me and all of the travel, that dark cloud just wouldn't seem to go away. My soul had a hole in it that I was looking to fill. I was still feeling damaged and was extremely fearful that if anyone either really knew me or found out who I really was, what was in my past, then I would be rejected.

So I started going to church. That should fix me. I had been to church when I had initially been in rehab two years earlier and I liked the feeling it gave me. I found a place down in Orange County near my parents' home: South Coast Community Church. Tim Timmons, the pastor, had a way of delivering a sermon by using everyday living with humor to translate into some spiritual message. At least that's what I heard.

I would party in Los Angeles on Saturday night and drive down Sunday morning, slightly hung over, and sit by myself in this extremely large and crowded facility. It was really labeled a New-Wave style church back then. Nothing stuffy and 100–200 people at every service. It was also a place to be seen in Newport Beach. Every Sunday I noticed the same 450SL Mercedes parked in the exact same spot. Black with red interior with the top down and "STEVE" on the license plate. Always right in front and in the same spot, as if he was the first person to get there.

Dona Speir

Not long after attending services there, I noticed this extremely well dressed, well-manicured usher who passed the plates every Sunday. He had said hello a few times and I had noticed an accent. This was Steve. He taught in the children's ministry and was very well liked. He was also a high-paid personal trainer and he was *very* good-looking. (I was now divorced from Rick, the drug dealer).

Our first date was at the Beach House in Laguna Beach. I had taken an apartment in Costa Mesa by then, thinking that moving back home to Orange County might help my soul sickness. Also, being closer to my parents did my heart good. I remember, on our way out of the restaurant, Steve stopped me before the valet parkers. He told me I had something on my eye. I faced him and started to shut my eyes, so he could see what it was. He kissed me. It was the sweetest moment.

We became inseparable. Everywhere we went we were called "Ken and Barbie." His striking good looks and tan muscular body with my model figure and long blonde hair made us an easy target for comments like that. We were the gorgeous young couple. His strong German accent gave him an even more exotic vibe.

The months went by and we got closer. I was doing a photo shoot in Sacramento (of all glorious spots) when, in the middle of the night, I had a knock on my hotel room door. It was Steve. He had driven all night and proposed to me. I was shocked. It took me by surprise. I said yes. Honestly I'm not even sure why. We weren't madly in love. I think most of Steve's friends were getting married and he felt the pressure. I just met his requirements. I, on the other hand, was still floundering in life, unhappy, insecure, and without too much direction. Looking back, I never really "planned" any of my life, never had any forethought, just went with whatever people around me thought was a good idea. My only real plan I ever had was to be a florist and here I was in Sacramento, a model.

And so, about seven months after we met, I was married at 21, walking down the same aisle where I first saw him with his collection plates. Technically, this was my third marriage. (In addition to Rick, I also had gotten "married" to the late actor Dennis Cole during a drunken weekend in Mexico. Though it was in a church, neither of us ever officially acknowledged the service. I know, it sounds crazy, because it was). He was part of the Newport Beach social scene and we fell right into that. At least I fell right into that with him. Although I always felt extremely insecure, because all of his friends had graduated college and had come from exceptionally better families than me. I had not even graduated high school.

At this time, my face was starting to appear everywhere. I was doing television, making all kinds of appearances, modeling for various ads, and we became *the* hot young couple of Orange County high society. Black tie events, VIP events, social columns, and all that goes along with that. It was uncomfortable for me. His mom, who was such a beautiful young woman, coached me along the way. I loved his family and the world seemed better than it had been before I met him.

Then, as quickly as this whirlwind relationship started, it began to fade. Steve started losing interest in me and I didn't know why or what to do. We never really had a deep friendship or any sort of foundation for marriage. I was on the road constantly. And my drinking began to escalate even more. We began to argue about everything while I was home. I had become volatile. I had skipped anger and gone right into rage. He had begun to withhold emotions if I didn't do what he wanted. I just wanted to come home and be loved. He was all of a sudden feeling financial burdens, which meant I needed to be on the road making more money. It was a vicious cycle.

On the road, I started heavy drinking and seeking out male attention. It was never his fault that the hole inside of me was so big. Tensions got very hot with us. I began to hate him. His new nickname became "Hitler," which I called him to his face, and even in front of his friends. It was because he struck me as so strict and German, but it was wrong. It was cruel. I was heartless at this stage of my life and I feel terrible looking back. As usual I started losing control. I started taking on boyfriends. I think he knew what I was up to and he resented me, but I didn't know what to do. I even asked his father for advice about why he was no longer interested in me, but his dad (who I loved dearly) didn't know what to tell me. Again, his boredom or whatever it was gave me an excuse to run wild. And run wild I did.

I was seldom home. When I was home, I was throwing things at him and putting holes in the wall. In the meanwhile, he was spending money we didn't have. And lots of it.

I did not pay attention to him or lend emotional support; I only drank heavily and had affairs.

I remember coming home from 26 days straight on the road to find him so excited to share that he bought two Porsches and they were in the garage. He was disappointed I wasn't excited because my first thought was I needed to go back out on the road and make more money. I had become very tired by then. He was spending far more than we were bringing in. When I started questioning about the finances (which he was in charge of) I was always told there wasn't enough. One morning after coming in from the road he woke me up to go sign some important papers. We went to an attorney's office and I signed them, trusting him thoroughly, only to find later I had signed Power of Attorney over to him.

As if things couldn't get worse in my life, I always have to run them into the ground. I was extremely drunk one afternoon after an event at "Hitler's" work. It was a beautiful afternoon and I was driven home by a friend of a friend. I had become semi belligerent at "Hitler's" event, so it was best I went home. Being left alone and to my own devices, I wandered next door and got friendly with the neighbor, someone who had not only been in our wedding party, but was also one of "Hitler's" college buddies. He was a slight partier, but nothing in comparison to me. He had been home watching sports and drinking beer. I gave myself to him, adding more into my bag of shame that had become so heavy by then. Just another innocent bystander in my wake of destruction.

Somewhere in this hellhole I had crossed the line from wanting an occasional drink to needing a drink. Big difference. I remember the day vividly. I was driving on my normal 60-mile trek from LA back home that night. I hadn't waited as I usually did for traffic to die by spending my time at the mansion having cocktails. By now I had made very good friends with the butlers at the mansion and they were always more than willing to go down into the wine cellar and pull out the "good stuff." The pressure was off for Playmate of the Year and hanging out had become no big deal. In fact, I was going up to the mansion many nights before I had to work the next day, and would go out drinking with friends. When "Hitler" would call looking for me, the butlers would always cover, saying they couldn't find me on the grounds and would take messages, knowing darn well my comings and goings were always logged.

So that night, driving home, a weird sensation came over me. I needed a drink. I needed to get home and have a drink. We had a bar set up in the house, but I never really touched it. The decanters had come from "Hitler's" mom from Germany. They had eventually been filled with hard liquor that I didn't drink. I kept mostly to wine and champagne for some reason. That night when I got home I mixed myself a drink of vodka and a mixer. I was careful to put it into a regular glass to hide my drinking from "Hitler." From then on that was the new norm: drinking at home and hiding my alcohol from my husband.

I was living a double and even triple life again. I had become an incredible liar. I was like a circus player, holding my sticks while keeping my plates in the air spinning. "Hitler" was booking trips with my agent while I was on the road to make more money, which fueled my bad behavior. It was a horrible cycle.

There were times when "Hitler" would call my hotel rooms in different states and other people would answer. It wasn't that I was in a romantic position; I simply had the hotel bar follow me back to my room and the party was going strong. Someone just answered the phone and couldn't find me. The next day I would find "Hitler" at the bottom of the stage after I was done signing autographs, explaining it took him three planes to get to Beaumont Texas.

Or I would get a phone call while shooting late in Los Angeles, him asking me if anyone ever drank champagne out of my belly button. I would always deny everything.

He insisted I was on NBC Nightly news. They were doing a special on bad behavior in the record industry and "Everyone saw it." I always insisted it was bad breaks and misunderstandings.

But the topping on the cake of my final self-destruction was a slow burn that eventually hurt more people than I care to admit. I had an affair with another friend of ours. Socially, we did a lot with this guy and his wife. It started when he touched me in Hawaii. I had been drinking from my own wine bottle at the pool. I had gotten extremely sunburned and in order to continue to be in the sun I had to drink to stop the pain. It made perfect sense to me at the time. The three of them had left me and I had attained my own white wine bottle from somewhere, carefully hiding it from the cocktail waitresses at The Hyatt Regency Maui.

When the three returned, for some reason I needed to make a phone call and Mr. X (as he will be called here) followed me back up to

Dona Speir

my room. I sat myself on the bed and he reached over and touched my back while I was on the phone. Though nothing happened that trip, it left the door wide open, creating a path of destruction that is still being talked about to this day in those tiny Orange County neighborhoods. Though the affair was not long, it was very destructive for the both of us.

I remember him saying to me, "All I have to do is give you alcohol," and he was right.

Finally, someone who understood! He was attentive and available and married to one of my girlfriends. But he gave me all the alcohol and attention I wanted.

I could tell him how unfairly treated I was at home and he would agree. I could call him from places on the road devastated about some imaginary problem and he'd show up. I think he liked being a hero and I know I needed something. I always needed something and more of it.

My problem was, there just never was enough of what I needed. Because my need was more. My impressions and expectations about men had been so corrupted so early in my life that I had no idea what was healthy and what was destructive. I had been robbed of that.

Chapter Nineteen
"Dona Hamilton" is Born

Obviously, at this point in my life any semblance of order was completely thrown out the window. I had returned to my previous ways of running out of control while not caring what kind of destruction I left behind me.

My March 1984 issue of Playboy coincided with the video revolution that was taking place. There was a company in Orange County called Karl-Lorimar which became very successful after producing the series of breakthrough videos by Jane Fonda. We are talking serious '80s culture. Karl really liked me and started talking to me about potentially doing a line of videos for them. I had done some television at that point but I was hardly what you could call an actress. I had appeared on the *New Mike Hammer* TV series, and I had done a few episodes of *Matt Houston* as well as a few bit parts in some cheesy movies. But again, nothing that you would call true acting. I never considered myself an actress despite the fact that there were people trying to push me on camera more and more. I liked modeling, but standing in front of a camera and actually talking? That was not for me. At least, not in my head.

Video was starting to become a pretty big deal and so of course Playboy got very involved. Playboy, as a company, was always looking out for the next big thing. They were very smart that way. So they created something called the *Playmate Playoffs*, which was a campy, very suggestive "sports" competition featuring two all-girl teams. So stupid, in my book. The girl teams competed in a variety of activities, all of which had them shaking their breasts, and, in my opinion, looking idiotic. I might have taken my clothes off for money, but I'd be damned if I would ever ride a mechanical bull in a half top and shorty shorts. They approached me initially because I was very athletic and a newer Playmate. They knew by my Playmate video (which was in my contract) that I was a waterskier, a runner, a volleyball player, and an all-around athlete. Basically anything they threw at me I would be able to do, and do well. And I told them flat out that there was no way I was doing it. Why not? Well, to me it seemed demeaning and pointless. I understood why Playboy was doing it; it made sense for them to package up competitions like this, and find new subjects for videos, but it just wasn't for me. I had zero interest and I had no problem telling him that. They offered a lot of money to the girls, lots of incentives, full-length mink coats to the winners, car phones (which was a huge expense back then), and tons of other prizes.

Playmate Playoffs. Right place at the right time.
This is how my film career started.

But then something happened. On day one of the two-day shoot up at the Playboy mansion, one of the girls got injured. I received a desperate call late Saturday night from one of the producers, begging me to come fill in. I really didn't want to do it, but they basically offered me whatever I wanted. They were desperate.

"Dona, you name it and we will do it."

At that point, "Hitler" had some business acquaintances that had been bothering him for a trip to the Playboy Mansion. Anything to see the girls. This was the perfect opportunity. Twenty playmates in bikinis running around playing games. It was a bucket list thing before the term even existed. *Okay, I thought, okay, maybe this is the chance where I can get everybody off my back, make some money, and get in good with the production company.* Well, it all worked out. I was able to bring up about ten people to visit the mansion, which was completely unheard of. No security checks, just bring them up. They paid me just what I asked for and made every accommodation for me. And so that's why the next day we all found ourselves up in Los Angeles at the Playboy mansion. It was a public relations job for me. It didn't matter if I won or lost. It didn't matter if I even really tried. Just show up in a bikini and smile. That's exactly what I did.

As it turned out, the production itself wasn't all that bad. I even had some fun doing it. The truly ironic thing was I ended up being on the cover of the video box, which I then went on tour for to help promote. Seems I'm always in the right place at the right time.

My life also changed that day because of somebody who was visiting the mansion to watch the festivities that were being videotaped. Sometimes life can change all because of one person who happens to be watching what you're doing. That's happened to me so many times in my life. Considering I wasn't supposed to be there at all, this was really something special.

His name was Andy Sidaris. If you've ever seen a sporting event on TV in the past 60 years, then you know the "Sidaris style." It all started when he took a part-time job at Dallas TV station WFAA-TV in the late '50s while still a college student. He quickly found himself in charge of directing the station's original programming, most notably sports coverage. He revolutionized the visual presentation of sports on television, particularly football, where he was the first to utilize hand-held cameras on the field to bring the audience closer to the action. Foreshadowing what he would go on to do later in his career, Sidaris also instituted the practice of inserting shots of cheerleaders during lulls in the game. It became known as "the honey shot."

As sports became a bigger part of TV in the '60s, Sidaris was hired by both NBC and ABC to train their staffs in his unique brand of cinematography, and he later joined ABC full time as the first director of their Wide World of Sports program. He remained an innovator of sports coverage for many years.

But he also loved filmmaking. His first feature was 1969's *The Racing Scene*, a documentary on auto racing that featured groundbreaking camerawork. Sidaris would go on to make *Stacey!* in 1973 and *Seven* in 1979, neither of which did much business. But then he hit on something that worked. With 1985's *Malibu Express*, he introduced what became his unmistakable formula—beautiful people filmed in exotic locations with an unapologetic amount of explosions, gunplay, all with big budget productions values…and lots of hot Playboy Playmates in sexy outfits.

I must have caught his eye that day at the mansion, because within just a couple of days I got a call from Andy's office offering me a part and his next film which was called *Hard Ticket to Hawaii*. Me. The lead. I would be portraying a tough, gun-toting federal drug enforcement agent named Dona Hamilton. Little did I know that this was the birth of my B-movie film career, a cult collection of seven features that I would work on through the early '90s. But first I had to get through film number one, at a time when I was drinking heavily.

My first meeting with Arlene Sidaris, Andy's wife, was extremely difficult. She was the producer of all the films. Though very funny, and beautiful, she was all business, watching every dime of production money. She was the bad cop while Andy played the good cop. When I first arrived at their home, I was offered a drink by their maid, and, though I really needed one, I chose apple juice. I was terribly intimidated by their Trousdale Estate home. It was way above Sunset Boulevard up in the heart of Beverly Hills. Looking over their tennis court, Arlene and I sat and had a chat and she handed me a script to read. She read the opposing characters.

As I read, I made no sense. I jumbled words and confused everything. I broke out in a sweat and was shaking.

Arlene seemed sweet but concerned. "I'm sorry to put you through that."

My response was, "It's okay, I'm used to it, it always happens." I was honest.

I hated reading, I hated being judged, and I always panicked.

I took an enormous drink of my apple juice and spit it back in my glass, spraying most of it all over her glass kitchen table. It was a disaster. I wanted to crawl into a hole. I knew this was a mistake. The maid had given me chicken stock by accident. It was oily and disgusting.

There was no way I would work for them. This was the exact reason I didn't want to be an actress. *I wasn't one.* I had no training, I was just a girl who was from Fountain Valley, and if you really knew about my past, you wouldn't hire me anyway.

I had lied to Arlene about being a fitness nut, telling her I could lead aerobic classes in Hawaii and teach about health and fitness. "Hitler" was in the health industry and I figured I could get way with pretending I was in his business. I was neither working out nor eating healthy. I was deep in my alcoholism and I was trying to hide it. Going to Hawaii was going to be the break I needed. "Hitler" was on my ass about my drinking and I was currently in a secret affair with a man I had no business being with.

Somehow, for some strange reason, I was given the role.

My first night in Hawaii did not go as planned—the first of many that would go poorly. I sat down at the outside bar before sunset and ordered some pu pu platters and a drink. It was roughly 4:00 p.m. The crew had already flown in earlier that week and we were to start filming the following morning. Makeup call 7:00 a.m. Breakfast 6:00 a.m.

My first night in Hawaii, I started drinking by the pool,
and got very drunk, trying to wear the same lei as my costar.

As I sat with my drink order, the crew and cast members came up one at a time. Everyone was happy and excited about being there. I was happy about being away from "Hitler." I started buying a drink or two and I must have blacked out or something. The next thing I remember is waking up with a tremendous hangover, not remembering where I was but seeing a ceiling fan going round, the daily call sheet on my bed. I looked at the clock and then outside. I dragged my ass out of the bed, realizing I had time. I put on my bathing suit and walked into the ocean to try to get rid of my hangover. It never failed. Always on the most important days of my life I was either drunk or so hungover I couldn't function. I was mildly trembling and I needed to eat. Not remembering much, I showered and dried my hair, grateful that that was all I needed to do. I walked into breakfast, ate, and went to makeup.

Within hours I was on location, ready for my first shot of the day. As I was being introduced to the DP (director of photography), I told him it was nice to meet him and I looked forward to working with him. The director of photography is the most important person to get along with on set. He will either make you look great or terrible. So when I told him how nice it was to meet him, I meant every word I said. He told me we had already met and that I bought him drinks last night. I knew this was going to be a long six weeks.

I held it together the best I could for a girl with secrets. My boyfriend insisted he come and visit. I think that was when my "good girl" cover was blown. That and the next time I showed up on set completely drunk.

It was the biggest night of production. The crew had been filming out on the island all day and I was to be filming an early night scene in the hotel restaurant. Because they were running so late, my call time got pushed back and back and back. I spent the day on the beach. It's not like there's a lot to do in Molokai. It started out with two beers. Which lead to two more, which lead to the six-pack. And then I don't remember.

It must have been close to 10:00 p.m. by the time I arrived on set. I had been drinking since noon. The makeup artist didn't know what to do with me. I was fried from the sun and showed up drunk with a cocktail in hand. The restaurant was filled with extras. The crew was on triple overtime. Everywhere I turned I saw a table of extras sitting looking either excited or bored. Then there were the dancers on the dance floor who had waited all day for their call. For they had been on call, too. They were tired and overworked. I was sunburned and drunk. Close to falling down drunk. I could barely stand in my heels.

I remember hearing "Action." All I had to do was walk in, hit my mark and lighting, and deliver my lines. I couldn't hit my mark. Time after time. If I hit my mark, I staggered out of the lighting. Then I couldn't get my lines out clearly. Then, when I did, I would roll my eyes up when I was done. It was a disaster and everyone knew their "star" was drunk on set. I couldn't walk or talk. I couldn't be left unsupervised. That night I cost the production company more money than I care to admit. We wrapped somewhere close to 4:00 a.m.

My saving grace besides the editor was that in my contract I had a pre-booked modeling gig in Oregon in two days. I was flying off the island for six days. I could take my show on the road. By then people were sick of me and I could run. It really was what I did best.

I slept all the way to San Francisco International Airport. That was after drinking heavily in the Oahu airport. It was a relief to be around other people who were excited to see me. I shot a cover of a large trucking magazine. I remember I had become at least ten pounds overweight from the alcohol consumption and the sun had bleached my hair almost white. There was nothing sexy about this shoot. I was stuffed in daisy dukes and we were staying in motor homes in a real abandoned ghost town. I flew for two days, drove for two days, and shot for two days.

On the last day of shooting, I had to sit on an authentic plank sidewalk left over from the 1880s. It left small splinters in my cheeks and thighs. They hurt but I didn't really think much of it.

After the long drive back to San Fran, I was staying in a beautiful hotel overnight and I remember thinking I just wanted to go home. Back to Newport. There I was, in a gorgeous hotel suite looking over San Francisco Bay, every amenity in the world. Once again my skin crawling. I couldn't stand to be alone. Facing myself was more than I could bear. I was desperately reaching for something. I had done so much harm everywhere. There was no place for me to be comfortable. Especially alone. Even for one night. "Hitler" didn't want me to fly home overnight. I hadn't been home in four weeks. My flight to Hawaii wasn't until late afternoon tomorrow. I was scared. I didn't want to finish the

Dona Speir

film. I had made so many problems for myself because of the drinking and the inability to act.

The crew was tired of me, the cast was tired of me, and I didn't want to face them. I ordered up a bottle of wine and called my boyfriend. He flew up immediately. I needed comfort, attention, and alcohol. Lots of alcohol. Mr. X was there within hours.

The first day back on set, I was to shoot my one and only "love" scene. It wasn't really a love scene. Mostly just the male lead and me making out. They would however get to film my breasts and my bottom. I'm not sure how I went from refusing to do the Playmate Playoffs to doing partial nudity, but here I was. I went into makeup, which included body makeup, and that's when they discovered the splinters.

All hell broke loose and next thing you know I was standing on a chair bent, over having makeup pulling splinters out of my ass. Always a problem. Decisions needed to be made if we could continue filming and stay on schedule.

No one was happy, especially me.

Around this time, I had also starting passing out from my drinking. The first time this happened I was on the road in Lake Charles, Louisiana, doing an appearance for Playboy. I was about to leave to go home when I received a call from a girlfriend of mine who was in New Orleans. It was a Saturday morning and she invited me down for Super Bowl Sunday. There was also something going on in New Orleans with the television industry and she said it would be exciting. Lake Charles didn't have many flights to New Orleans so somehow I caught a private plane and within hours I was there. Unfortunately, I had forgotten to tell "Hitler" that I wasn't coming home. I had been up all night partying and never went to bed the night before. When I arrived at my hotel room, someone knocked on the door. They had two hands full of drugs. One with downers and one with cocaine. He told me to choose one. I chose the downers, knowing damn well the cocaine would kill me. I immediately took the downers, thinking I could sleep for six hours.

I took a 30-minute nap and heard another knock on the door. This time it was the warning that it was time to roll. Once again in my '80s getup I was out the door, angora fur and rhinestones flying behind me.

Not knowing who was in the limousine with me, I continued the party from the night before.

We finally landed at a very lively place with a live band and it was packed. I mean packed. Wall to wall people. We got inside and there I was with a more charming intellectual guy with zany hair, who turned out to be Kelsey Grammer. We wrapped his scarf around both our necks and were trying to walk like conjoined twins in the bar, laughing hysterically. The people were parting like the Red Sea. The younger guy in front, though not as tall as the guy I was with, was making quite a stir with the girls. The young girls were screaming with delight as Woody Harrelson parted the way for Kelsey Grammer and me. I had never seen *Cheers* and was clueless. It really didn't matter to me. I was having the time of my life. Laughing and playing. He was hilarious.

Bar after bar, club after club, Kelsey and I went in tied together. As the night wound down, all of the party (which was a few limos full) ended back at Kelsey's suite. He asked me what I wanted to drink, and they roared off to pick up some more liquor. While up in the suite I remembered I hadn't called "Hitler" to tell him not only was I not coming home, but I had moved locations. I saw a phone on a wall which had the perfect and sweetest little purple velvet settee underneath. As I swayed down the hall to the phone with all intentions of calling, taking a little rest seemed like a good idea. I must have passed out cold. I guess someone thought I was chilly because they laid their coat on me. I remember cuddling up underneath it. Pulling it up to my chin. The next guest came in and laid their coat on me as well.

Kelsey Grammer and me out partying in New Orleans.
Another blur of an evening.

I'm assuming the party went on, the guests thinking this was the spot to drop your coats. The party was in full swing when I eventually came to, buried deep beneath what felt like 300 pounds of wool, completely sweaty and with my little angora sweater stuck to my face. I sprung out of the coats like a jack-in-the-box.

From down the hall I heard Kelsey's voice. "There you are! I've been looking all over for you."

With a full smile, we resumed our partying as if all of this was normal.

I was a mess.

Chapter Twenty
My Last Drink

March 13th was like any other day. I had gained quite a bit of weight from my drinking and felt sluggish. "Hitler" and I were constantly at odds. He had been working early Saturday morning while I slept in from Friday night's shenanigans. Nothing unusual. About this time, I noticed I was waking up in the middle of the night. Not just stirring, but wide-awake, totally wired, ready to go somewhere. It was disturbing and startling. It was later I found out this was common. My blood sugar had dropped from my large intake of alcohol. If I had only known then a drink in the middle of the night would have cured that.

Saturday afternoon rolled around and it was reason enough to go out. I met a girlfriend for happy hour, or, in reality, a couple of drinks. It had stopped being happy years ago. I had promised "Hitler" I would come home to make dinner. Odd, considering I didn't cook. But I was willing to say anything to get out of the house. El Ranchito Restaurant was a little local spot a few blocks from my house. This wasn't their main restaurant, but it always did in a pinch. It was owned by two brothers, one of whom was usually there and always happy to see me. Around this time, not everyone was. After about two hours I think I'd had around six Long Island Iced Teas with Denise (I think that was her name. Funny, she had become my best friend in the entire world, and I'm not sure of her name). She and I got to doing what I liked best: husband bashing. I'm not sure if she was bashing hers but I'm certain I was bashing mine, which in turn justified my next brainstorm: going out on the town for a Saturday night, naturally without my husband. He was trying to monitor my alcohol intake and it was always a screaming match. Me screaming, and him being defeated by my bad behavior.

Somehow I drove to my house and put on *that* outfit. A tight black skirt, tied-up top, high heels, false eyelashes, and giant eighties hair.

Once again, "Hitler" wasn't impressed. In fact, as usual, we got into one of our common driveway fights. The neighbors had become accustomed to this behavior and had stopped bringing it up. It was the type of influence I had brought into their neighborhood. Living on either side of our condo now were his college friends. I had stopped caring about what they thought or said. At least I tried to believe I did. When I drank, I couldn't control my behavior, so my best defense was to pretend I didn't care. Deep inside, I was burning with guilt and shame. The only relief was to continue drinking.

By the time I got into my "out on the town" costume, I was out in the driveway arguing with "Hitler" about taking the car. Once again I was downright drunk and driving under the influence, him trying to get me to hand over the keys, not wanting me to kill someone or myself, me yelling that he was always trying to control me.

Getting behind the wheel to pick up my girlfriend with "Hitler" imploring me not to take the car, I rolled down the window and said, "No, I'm leaving," in a drunken slur.

In a last-ditch effort by my husband to do the right thing, he stood behind the bumper of the car. "Dona, I am not moving. Get out of the car, you're drunk! You are not driving!" he yelled in his heavy accent.

"I told you to move. I'm leaving."

"Dona, you're not taking the car."

"I told you."

And with that last comment, I slammed the car in reverse, and hit him.

While he was limping out of the way, I roared down the driveway without even a glance back.

I don't remember where I met up with my girlfriend, but I do remember I lost her that night. It was somewhere between two Red Onion bars. Sunset Beach or Long Beach. Most of the night is vague and what I do remember I wish I didn't. I'm sure we had been drinking or dancing, though the memory is foggy. I recall talking to her in a parking lot near some bushes. And then poof. She was gone. I've never seen her since. It's apparent she couldn't keep up with me, and, if you got in the way of my drinking, you were left behind. It's been 32 years since I've seen her. I still don't know what happened to her that night.

My next memory was on the dance floor at a place in Long Beach, happy as I've ever been, the cocktail waitress bringing me drink after drink on the floor. Not dancing with anyone in particular, just dancing. Then hearing that terrible sound of doom. The one that send shivers down my spine: "Last call"

I had been drinking solidly since approximately 4:30 p.m. and it was now 1:30 a.m. I knew I needed to sober up to drive home so I ordered a Baileys Irish Cream and coffee. Baileys liquor, which reminded me of fluoride toothpaste (which I found out immediately), and coffee, which I wasn't in the habit of drinking. It all made perfect sense to me at that time.

I drank my drink and did what I always did: went home with the manager.

I had known him socially for a while from frequenting his bar. I knew he had a crush on me, and, at 1:30 a.m. on a Saturday night, I'm sure anyone looked good to him. I don't know how he ended up driving my car but the next memory is being at his home. I remembered always trying to call "Hitler" whenever it got late. By now, I also had the habit of passing out.

Seemed that every time I went to phone him, I just fell asleep, no matter where I was, and this was no exception. It was always at the end of the night after a long drinking spree and I was always calling drunk with an excuse which was always a lie.

My last recollection of that night was seeing the manager's phone on his nightstand and thinking about calling home.

When I came to in the manager's bed, my head was at the wrong end of the bed. I have no memory of what happened. Most of my clothes were still somewhat on and I was groggy, my mouth dry. I could barely swallow. I looked outside and was grateful to see my car. I didn't know what city I was in but I knew I needed to get home and come up with an excuse.

When I arrived home, there he was, sitting in front of the condo on the porch, waiting to go to church. The memories began to flood back to me. I got out of the car. My '80s hair had creased to one side, I had a hole in the knee of my black stockings, my false eyelash was half stuck to my cheek, and I was filled with shame and guilt and remorse. Trembling inside but filled with defiance.

I walked by him, took a Valium from the medicine chest, and got into bed, still somewhat dressed.

Several hours later, when my husband returned from church, he sat on the bed next to me and said he knew everything. The neighbor, the friend, and much more. I had no idea how he found out. Then came that fucking question. The question he had asked me over Valentine's Day in Austria, one month prior. The issue, the elephant in the room, the reason I hated him so much.

We had been on a two-week ski trip with his parents. We surprised them in Berlin and then went skiing in Austria. I drank the entire trip, all day and all night. I drank all night in the pub, then drank on the slopes, then in the restaurant, then back in the pub. It was there I began drinking in the mornings. I hated skiing. I hated the cold. It was the little grey chalet I couldn't wait to get to. It called me and haunted me. I couldn't wait to get there in the morning.

I had to do a few ski runs every morning first, and then say, "Let's warm up."

In the grey chalet was a warm red wine concoction called Gilhwein, a hot red wine with sugar and one or two almonds floating on top. I needed it. I craved it. That dreaded morning drink I had heard about from those old drunks in rehab. I was drinking 24/7, completely around the clock. Not realizing I was taking that ever-present morning drink. Just believing I was doing what skiers do. Then the strangest of all phenomena happened: I couldn't get drunk and I couldn't get sober. I had so much alcohol in my system I had reached that point I had heard about in rehab. Fuck. And if things couldn't get worse. Out came *that* question.

Sitting next to me on the bed at the ski lodge he asked me, "What are you going to do about your drinking?"

Now, back home in the cold morning light one month later he asked me again. "What are you going to do about your drinking?"

I was in fight or flight mode. I was scared, angry. Who had he talked to? Who did this to me? How did he know everything? Fuck him. *I'm done with this shit* was my immediate thought. (Never taking responsibility for my behavior.) While on the road, if he couldn't find me, I always had an excuse for staying out all night, and he could never prove it, but not coming home and hitting him with the car was an entirely different situation.

My world was crashing, and I was completely out of excuses. I didn't have any. My brain was foggy. I wanted to run. I hated myself. I hated him. I hated everything and everybody. The town I lived in, everyone who knew my secrets, there wasn't enough alcohol to cover my pain and the Valium wasn't doing it. I was dying inside. The despair was incredible. I was completely bewildered how it had gotten to this point. I was entirely alone in this enormous world and no one understood. No one to run to. The gig was up. I was cornered, and I was pissed. It was submit and die. And I needed a drink more than ever right then.

"I'm going to go to AA." It flew out of my mouth before I could catch it. I hated AA. I had no intention of getting sober. It was another lie. I wanted to get away from him.

My next thought was, *I'll get "good" for 90 days, clean up my reputation. Everyone will feel sorry for me, and then I'll divorce him. I can do what I've always done.*

"I'll go to a meeting tonight," I said, with no intention whatsoever of stopping my drinking.

My husband took me to a meeting that night. I cried the entire time. Not because I felt a part of it, but because I was busted. I shared with the group that I had once had a year of sobriety and that I had been drinking for three and a half years. Poor little me. So full of myself, and self-pity. Looking for my husband to get off my back and feel sorry for me. No intention whatsoever of quitting my drinking. It was the husband who had to go.

I stood up and said, "My name is Dona and I'm an alcoholic." I was crying crocodile tears, putting on an entirely false "boo-hoo-hoo" act to make everybody believe what I was saying. But it was a selfish scheme to get out of there as quickly as I could. I was hung over and being dramatic. I figured I could trade on self-pity to make the whole thing go away.

Dona Speir

Chapter Twenty-One
The First Year of Sobriety

March 1987 marked the first year without a drink...what can I say? It sucked...just flat-out sucked. Even though I was making progress at meetings, losing drinking was like losing my security blanket, my lover, and my best friend all at once in one horrific accident. Gone. Just like that.

Facing this wreckage I had created without my pacifier was horrible. There was nothing pleasant about it. Not to mention, I needed a major perception tweak. I was still an extremely sick young girl. The second day after I had stopped drinking, "Hitler" decided it was a grand idea to confront Mr. X. Great timing! Just what I needed. He threatened him that if he wouldn't meet him at his place of business he would go to his home and tell his wife. Awesome. By noon on day two of no drinking, as if life couldn't get any worse, "Hitler" had taken the driveway screaming party to a new home. All three of them, Mr. X, Mrs. X, and my husband were standing outside of Mr. X's home yelling like maniacs that day. I did a drive by and decided I wasn't stopping. Mrs. X was yelling at me from the distance. *Fuck, I stopped drinking for this?* Who needed these headaches?

I didn't know what to do or where to go when I drove away. I went to a noon meeting that day during this crisis. I drove straight there. I pulled this little old lady out of the meeting and told her what was going on. She told me it would be all right and to come in and take a seat. I have no idea why but I did. And it helped.

I had been going to 7:00 a.m. meetings every day. Just to get out of the house and away from my husband. The guilt was eating me alive. I actually started liking the meetings. The people there were supportive. They listened to me. And they wanted to help me. They actually had my back.

I had not had a valid driver's license for three years. In that time, I had accumulated four warrants for my arrest. When I talked about this during the meetings, a group of the people there decided to go with me so that I could get my license back. They came with me to Los Angeles, San Diego, Riverside, and also Orange County so that I could go, pay off what I owed, and take responsibility for my actions. Within a few months, I got my license back. That meant a lot to me. Nobody judged me at these meetings. Nobody shamed me. For the first time in my life, I was beginning to feel as if I belonged.

At 90 days without a drink I was shipped off to make my second film for the Sidaris series. Half of me was grateful to skip town—the other half was petrified. I had never really worked sober and I had created such disorder last time I was with the cast and crew. I wasn't making this film because they loved me so dearly. It was because it was becoming a series and I was the female star. I'm sure they had regretted it after the first film. They were stuck with me. The only reason it was able to work in the beginning was because of good editing. They were able to cut around my drunken stumbles and eye rolls. I knew facing the same crew I had fucked over so badly was going to be intense, and, because this was a low budget production, everyone, including me, needed the work. Showing up in Molokai, Hawaii for 30 days was incredibly painful. Making apologies to the producer for wasting their time and money was humbling. Apologizing to the crew for making them work extra-long days because of my drunken behavior sucked. Also, to the makeup artist for having to pick splinters out of my ass, and to everyone else I affected. It was extremely embarrassing. I just tried to be of maximum service to everyone on the set and stay out of the way. I spent a lot of time by myself on that trip. But in the end, I actually started feeling better because of the reactions I got to my apologies. People were forgiving, they were supportive, and I felt like they were rooting for me.

After 30 days in Hawaii I returned home and enrolled in some acting classes at a local theater. After about five lessons I returned to set to finish filming.

I had never taken an acting class in my life and after my first scene on set the Director of Photography said, "That was the best scene you have ever done, Dona. It was terrific."

I did it in one take and I remembered all my lines. I realize now that I didn't know what I didn't know. My commitment to getting better was starting to pay off. Maybe this didn't suck after all.

Back home, life had become very complicated for me in tiny Newport Beach as word had gotten out about the relationship between me and Mr. X. It was the talk of the town—a glittery, gossipy buffet. Not that all my other actions weren't. My husband and I were high profile anyway and this was just another problem Dona had made. I couldn't go anywhere without shame. It wasn't like I didn't feel like shit about myself anyways. I always have—there wasn't enough makeup in the world to hide behind—only I no longer had my bottle and everywhere I went I saw people rattling on about the scandal. I know "Hitler" was taking the brunt of it, but thankfully he never threw it in my face. He was always good about that. He didn't have to; I was beating the hell out of myself on a daily basis. I knew all my skeletons and it was a juggling game to try to remember all my lies. Even though I had stopped drinking, I still had lots of mopping up to do in my life.

One afternoon I was in the most popular hair salon in Newport getting cut by "The Guy." While I was in the shampoo bowl getting a luxurious massage, he bent over, looking me directly in the eye. With his deep French accent, he said, "I heard about your affair with Mr. X," smiling with a bit of satisfaction for being in the know. All the while never stopping shampooing nor breaking eye contact, no farther than ten inches from my face.

I was pinned. He knew it. I felt like a trapped bird. Wings broken. Completely demoralized. He had always been the one who used to say he cut the hair of an actress and a centerfold. Pictures of me on his station. And now he could say he got the information firsthand because I know people were asking.

Out of nowhere I opened my mouth and out came, "That's old news, you just heard about that nonsense?"

I shut him down completely. I realized at that moment that by owning my truth, no one in this entire world could ever harm me again, that I would own all my behaviors and beat others to the punch every time. I swore to myself, I would never ever try to hide who I was or what

I've done again. *Ever.* No one would ever be allowed to shame me without my permission. I walked out of that salon looking the world in the eyes, with a new fire and sense of confidence.

At six months sober, "Hitler" and I were done, ready for divorce, and not a second too soon. We split up. But what a life change. Gone was upscale Newport and it was back to my parents' house. Again. My dad gave me two weeks. Here I was, 23 years old, living in the bedroom with the rainbow wallpaper again, going through divorce number two and a half, not counting the sham marriage to a guy in Mexico on a drunken weekend. An actor. I'd rather not recount here as the entire thing was a farce. I had no money to speak of. I wasn't sure where the money had all gone. "Hitler" said we were broke and what money I owed on my Porsche was more than it was worth. I had never ever been in this situation. It was completely the opposite of everything my dad had taught me. All the information about the credit card rules and living within your means.

Having no money wasn't the biggest issue. I was 23 and I had forgotten how to balance a checkbook. All of those years as a little girl listening to my dad teach simple but valuable lessons seemed to be wasted. Trying to balance mine one morning, I got so frustrated I ripped it up and threw it in the fireplace. I had the living skills and emotions of a 14-year-old. I had no idea how to take care of myself in any way, how to grocery shop and feed myself well-balanced meals. I pretty much lived off microwave popcorn and scrambled eggs. The IRS was sending me letters that I was simply shuffling around, thinking they would disappear.

ATMs had just become popular. One afternoon the ATM ate my card. I was sure that the IRS cleared my bank account. Going to my father for help and explaining what happened, I gave him a diamond ring for collateral for a large sum of money, only to find out on Monday that the ATM was broken.

I was clueless about how things worked. When I couldn't find anything to wear, I would throw my clothes on the floor like a child and cry. I had dropped out of school at the end of the tenth grade. My only saving grace was I was always a reader and I read the newspaper every day since I was in the sixth grade.

I finally got into my own apartment, a studio with a Murphy bed. As usual I had already picked my next "winner," a guy from New York who lived in the same apartment building. How convenient. And what a train wreck. It was just another sick pattern. Like Rick, he had a girl in Canada whom he wouldn't let go of and whom I heard about constantly. It was extremely sick and toxic. While I was going through the divorce, I found that "Hitler" had hidden money and it eventually came back around to me. This would also be the new norm for me. Money issues and men. But at least I wasn't drinking (not that I wasn't tempted). Challenges were everywhere, but I kept going to meetings every day to try and save myself. *One day at a time*, I kept telling myself.

I started to get on my feet financially because I wasn't drinking. I was also traveling a great deal. That posed a new problem. *I'm now going to 12-step meetings and traveling to promote movies all over the world*, I thought. *What am I to tell these press people I do with my time? I'm in divorce court, in therapy, I owe the IRS money, I'm going to 12-step meetings, and doing decoupage?*

My one-year anniversary of not drinking came around. I was given a cake.

I blew out the candle and said, "If I knew it was going to be this hard...I would have kept drinking."

Dona Speir

Chapter Twenty-Two
The Beer Poster

After my divorce, the drama slowed down. I really didn't have much to do between going to 12-step meetings and interviews for modeling jobs and TV.

One day I started reflecting back on something. My mom had always been involved with volunteer work for one thing or another and had dragged me along as a child. That must have made some sort of impression on me because I found myself volunteering at the Salvation Army in Santa Ana. Only one afternoon a week. As time went on, it turned into a day or two, and, pretty soon, I was there for all of my spare time. My main job was checking vouchers for food and packing from their little pantry, handing out sacks of groceries, some filing, and lots of cleaning. I got to know the families and began to really like them. They kept telling me how grateful they were for me, but honestly I was just grateful I had something to do and somewhere to go. Besides cleaning up the wreckage of my past, there would be years of lesson learning and trying not to create more wreckage. It was a very narrow road I was walking on. My life had become very small while I was drinking. Now I was going to try to live life without hiding behind my occasional seven cocktails and do it graciously. Those families that came through and the people that trusted me as a volunteer will never know just how much they helped me as a person, how that simple reason for being helped got me through such a tough time.

My last year or so of drinking I had one wish. This may sound odd but all I wanted to do was land a beer poster gig. Pretty low goal considering all I had established. My thinking was, if I could land a national beer poster for Budweiser or Coors, they would put me on a poster-signing tour. I thought it would be fabulous, getting paid to go on tour, signing my name in bars, and drinking. My other thought was that "Hitler" could not be mad at me for disappearing all night while drinking. It was my job, after all. The ultimate goal in life for an alcoholic girl. I had been on so many interviews and the best I could do was land a one-time stand-up poster for Killian Red. Because they had computer generated my hair red they weren't particularly interested in putting me on the road. Damn.

As fate would have it, I did land that beer poster. Approximately three to five months after I quit drinking, I landed a national Tecate poster. Tecate beer. I would spend the next two and a half years running around signing Tecate Beer posters in every Mexican bar and restaurant that would take me. God always did have a sense of humor and it was apparent I had a big lesson to learn from this.

With fans at a Tecate Beer appearance.
Notice how far the beer is from my face!

While traveling through the west coast states signing for Tecate, I would arrive at up to six bars in one night, always to a waiting crowd with posters and photos in hand. By the time 9:00 p.m. came around, the crowds were rowdy and always drunk. As they leaned over to scream their names at me to write on their posters (because the music was always loud), they would occasionally spit and spill drinks on me, always slurring and trying to act charming while trying to pick me up. It's amazing what happens when you look yourself in the face. It was pretty ugly but funny at the same time. What I witnessed was an excellent experience of what I didn't want anymore. There wasn't anything out there for me any longer. The only thing I said I wanted was the Pope mobile to sit in, so they would quit spitting on me. By the time I was finished with my Tecate contract, I had literally taken thousands of pictures with a Tecate Beer can in my hand (usually unopened) and I never once took a single drink. Nor did I want to. Not one person ever knew. The crowds or my bosses. No one even noticed. The perfect gig.

Around this time, I was spending less and less time at the Playboy mansion. I had become an outsider with quite a few of the Playmates. I had begun to notice that when I walked up to a group of girls they would stop talking or move away from me. It could be I just didn't have anything in common with them anymore. I had told my agents that I had gotten sober and if at any time any of the girls needed help that they could call me. I was always available. Working with the Playmates without partying in the '80s had become a lonely business. It reminded me of how I had felt when I was young. Never fitting in. I didn't have friends in my social circle, I didn't have friends in my Playboy circle, and I really didn't have many sober friends because of how much I traveled. I was young and alone most of the time. But I was always grateful for my family. And I was finally starting to grow up.

Dona Speir

Chapter Twenty-Three
Once a Playmate...

Things at Playmate promotions had loosened up dramatically. Valerie Cragin was no longer running promotions and Lori Hart was in charge. I was finally sober for a semi-substantial period and now had a fairly good, responsible reputation. Though not many of the Playmates knew I was sober, it did create a weird vibe with the other girls. They seemed to keep walls between us, which was nothing new to me. There were a lot of drugs going around and I was not in the in-crowd. In fact, I was so far in the out-crowd that toward the end Lori Hart let me be the lead when she could not go on promotions because I was the next most responsible person.

One of my favorite clients came after a few years of working for Playboy. It was the Sands Hotel and Casino in Atlantic City. Every girl wanted this promotion. It could mean thousands of dollars a night. The Sands would hire us for their high rollers or what they called "Whales." We would come in for a fashion show for their wives on a Friday evening. The Sands had already done an enormous dinner with them and had a stage set up adjacent to the high roller suite. After the fashion show the wives seemed to disappear somewhere and we would have cocktails with the Whales. Though unspoken (between Playboy and the Casino), our job was to get the Whales to spend money on the casino floor.

Later that night, the men would gamble and we would be invited to the casino floor. That's when things got really weird. These high rollers would invite us over to gamble and party, tipping us when they won, generally $100 or $500 chips. Some of the girls came back with thousands and thousands of dollars. My first trip, I made quite a bit of money, which made me realize that the Sands could be a regular client, and that I wanted them long term. I began to focus on their management to ensure I would continually have employment, so instead of hustling for $100 chips by talking to drunk gamblers, I made sure I continually went back to the lounge where my boss was and got to know him and the entire crew. I was always uncomfortable gambling with these men anyway. It seemed rather pimpish. When I did have to gamble, I choose the sweetest older man, who always brought his son and his son's girlfriend. He would give me money to play craps (in which I had no idea what I was doing) and he just loved to explain the game in his New Jersey accent. After about 60 minutes (which was enough to keep my job), I would give the money I won to his son's girlfriend, because I felt like if I kept it, it would be akin to prostitution. Or that I owed someone something. (The bosses eventually caught wind of that through the cameras and loved me for it). I guess the family values stuck with me. My day rate from Playboy had been raised to $700 a day but I've always thought bigger. It was what my father had instilled in me.

On one particular trip to Atlantic City, Lori Hart couldn't make it, and, because I knew everyone, she asked me to keep an eye on the girls. There were a few new girls and no fashion show. Just dinner and gambling. At this point, after dinner, I no longer gambled; I changed out of my dress and put on my jeans and sneakers. I was making a quick round on the casino floor before bed. I was leaving in the morning to NYC to meet with two photographers for other business. The Whales who knew me by now were asking me who might be the one girl who would sleep with them. How stupid. The pit bosses were giving me the nod as I walked through. Then this particular high roller I was always dodging who was slightly handsy saw me and called my name across the floor. *Busted.* The pit boss saw me and I had no choice. The Whale insisted I play 21 with him. I was playing two hands at a time for $4,500 a hand. After I won a few hands of blackjack for him, he gave me a $500 chip and I disappeared. I was back up at my room by 1:30 a.m. and was asleep quickly thereafter. That's when all hell broke loose.

I was awakened by a call from Lori Hart. She had received a call from the head of Sands security. It seemed some of the girls who were gambling at the same table all night became completely inebriated. The Whales were waiting to see if the girls would sleep with them. The girls decided it was a good idea to pick up chips from the table (a *big* no-no, we were told that up front. We were only allowed to keep them if they were handed to us off the table) and put them in their cleavage. It was recorded on video. I got up and got dressed and headed back down. Whispering to these girls wasn't pleasant because they were drunk and denied it. Not long after confronting that issue, I had to go back upstairs to the boss's lounge and have a three-way call with Lori Hart. I wasn't 15 minutes in bed when my door flew open. I shared my room with another Playmate. She came in drunk with two high rollers and proceeded to change her clothes with the door open. I pretended to be asleep. It was for the best. It was a harsh reminder of why I quit drinking. In the morning I awoke to find $100 bills folded up all over the floor. They must have come out of her high heels. I remember thinking she would never remember if I kept them. Then my next thought was, *she worked hard for them.* I put them all back in her shoe, making sure she didn't know I saw them. It was the last time I worked for the Sands Hotel in Atlantic City. I just knew too much.

Dona Speir

Chapter Twenty-Four
No Exception to the Rule

June 26, 1988 I was in my apartment that I had moved into when "Hitler" and I divorced. I was a year and a half sober when I received a call from my mom. She insisted that I come home immediately. I knew it wasn't good. I begged my mom to tell me what was wrong on the phone. I could tell by her voice that something had happened.

"Your oldest brother died, please just come home."

My first thought was, *this is impossible.* There had always been six children. *Are you trying to tell me there are now five?* It just didn't compute in my brain. There was no way this could happen. How could there only be five?

When I arrived home to the only house I ever lived in, my mom and dad and oldest sister were there. My mom was on the phone, my sister Julie's face was completely red from crying, and I had never seen the look on my father that I did that day. I sat on the couch. It felt like things were moving in slow motion. Nothing was particularly clear. At first they were saying he had killed himself, and then they were saying he was murdered. I wasn't getting anything straight and neither were they. All we really knew was my brother was dead and he had been in a motel room in El Paso, Texas, alone.

He died alone.

It hit me like a ton of bricks. It shook me to my core. I wanted to throw up. I was the only one in the room that knew. I kept silent. I remembered from the last time I saw my oldest brother we had made insinuations about cocaine. He had every sign of being an addict/alcoholic. The four marriages, the unpaid child support, the disappearing from the family. I sat on the couch in shock. My oldest brother Scott, regardless of how he died, was a victim of drug and alcohol abuse. At the age of 38, he was dead.

He was the only other addict in our family. The oldest child and the youngest. There I sat, sober, on my parents' couch, watching my family come in one at a time, devastated. My three sisters sobbing. My other brother speechless. It was like I was in a movie. Scott had three children. Now, all of them were fatherless. I, on the other hand, chose to throw my life away and hurt other people without any regard. It was becoming clearer and clearer how incredibly selfish I was. Survivors' guilt was hitting me hard.

As it turned out, my oldest brother Scott was murdered in that hotel room that day. A single gunshot to his head. Someone had come in and cleaned out the room. There was no gun found, there was no alcohol or drugs found. No one ever knew how or why this happened. Those were the type of things that happen to other people, not to my family. Those are the kind of things I would read about in the Los Angeles Times. They didn't happen to people who lived on Walnut Street. Not with parents who had been married for almost 60 years. But those things do happen to people who don't stop drinking and using drugs. And it was the biggest influencer of my life. The fact that I am no exception to the rule hit home hard. If I didn't change my actions, I would die. There was absolutely nothing special about me in this entire world. And, I now thought, there was absolutely no reason whatsoever that anyone should die from drug addiction or alcoholism with the resources we have today.

For just the second time in my life, I saw my father drunk. The first was at his 25th wedding anniversary party. Scott was my father's oldest son and he really never recovered from this.

Less than a year after my brother had died, my parents put their home up for sale. All of my brothers and sisters had moved out of Orange County but me. I believe his death fractured our family deeper than anyone ever realized. My family home sold quickly and was boxed up fast. They were moving to Prescott, Arizona. I had no idea where that was. The day before the moving trucks came, I knew I needed to make things right with my father before he moved. *If I don't, I may never do it,* I thought.

It was a Sunday afternoon. I had done enough soul searching to know that everything I had done to him and in his home was wrong. In spite of my behavior, I knew the difference between right and wrong. It was bred in me. Despite the sexual abuse, the drugs, and everything else, there was no excuse for torturing my dad the way I had.

It was time to face reality. I walked into my father's bedroom. He was lying on his bed, boxes all around him. The little black and white television I used to watch Little House on the Prairie was sitting on the window ledge. The house felt strange. Dead. I knew it was an end and a beginning.

I swallowed hard and said, "Dad, I need to talk to you."

As I closed the door behind me, he sat up on the bed, aware that this was serious. "Okay, what is it, Dona?"

My mom came in almost immediately.

"Dona wants to talk to us."

"Actually, Mom, I want to talk to Dad," I corrected him. I wasn't ready to make amends to my mother yet. I was still doing the work I needed in regards to our relationship. It took me years to separate her issues from mine

Looking disgusted, she backed out and shut the door behind her. "What is it, honey?" he asked me, softer than he had been as of late.

The room was silent. I saw my father had aged.

"Dad, I need to tell you, I am so truly sorry for all the harm and pain I caused you and our family. You never deserved it. Not in the home you worked so hard to create. You were always good to me, treated me well, and took care of me the best you knew how. I am so very, very sorry. It was never intentional. I was a bad daughter and I was so wrong." The tears streamed down my face. All of a sudden, I missed those long afternoons when he was paying the bills and telling me stories about life.

"You need to know," I continued, "if there is anything I can do to make this right for you, to be a better daughter and to straighten anything out, I am more than willing."

My father looked old and worn, no doubt in part due to my behavior. Looking at me with tears in his eyes, he broke a long silence. "I have always loved you, Dona."

It was the first time my father ever said he had loved me. I was 26 years old. Years and years of pain fell away from me. That little girl lying in the ICU was no longer scared. She was finally becoming a grown woman; finally, after realizing what she had created and the harm she had done to the people she had loved the most in the entire world.

"I love you too, Daddy." I hugged my dad and he held me for a moment before my mom walked in. She stared at the both of us as we cried. That moment was all I had ever wanted in the entire world.

Chapter Twenty-Five
Right Place, Right Time

I was still making movies for Arlene and Andy Sidaris. I would go on to star in seven films total, most of them shot in Hawaii. I had even attained an agent there because I was there so frequently. I was learning to work smarter. But things changed on set for me. I was thoroughly grateful for the work. Malibu Bay Films was always good to me considering my first film and how bad I screwed up. From then it was always in my contract that I had access to a car to attend 12-step meetings. I'm sure the Sidaris's never wanted to see a drunk and sunburned Agent Dona Hamilton on set ever again and they were always more than supportive.

From then on I made sure I was a worker among workers and always pulled my weight on set.

The strange thing was the way the party crowd treated me now. Though not openly in recovery, it was known I didn't drink. Recovery was still not trendy in the early '90s. After shooting all day, they would see me hustling off to go to a meeting. I could hear them all at the bar:

"Hey, where's *she* going?

"Oh, her? She's off to one of those Triple A meetings."

Then everyone would break out in laughter. Feeling like a social outcast, I just tried to be kind to all. I had worked long enough with the cast and crew to know their family members. Because I had earned the reputation by now as reliable and everyone knew I was back in my hotel room early, I often received phone calls from the significant others of actors or crew members on set. They were calling looking for their better (or worse) halves. Trying to get me to spill what was happening while on location. Sometimes crying, sometimes begging. Then I would deny and have to call the players to have them get their significant others off my back. Tiptoeing around them on set. Seemed like night after night, film after film.

Affair after affair. Once again on the other side, I was seeing how hurt people hurt people, the mirror so closely shoved up my face that I was being forced to change.

There were the few who saw I was happier on set. I had changed, and I no longer was a slave to my past. Those individuals slowly but steadily buzzed around me like bees to honey and asked questions. They saw that I could laugh at my drinking blunders without being in full shame. Owning my truth was an attraction and they wanted to know more about it. I was beginning to understand that maybe I wasn't in the entertainment business for the sake of "my craft."

God knows I really didn't have a craft. I've always said I couldn't act my way out of a paper bag, and if you've ever seen my films or anything I've acted in, you'd probably agree.

What I was beginning to understand was that maybe I had a bigger purpose in life and maybe, just maybe, I went through all of what I did to share it with others. To relieve a little of their pain with some humor and love. That maybe, just maybe, my purpose or calling is much bigger than I am. It was like my days in the flower shop. My intuition was calling me.

To seal the deal on my purpose to help others through my non-talent talent, I went to Las Vegas to headline The Playboy Girls of Rock N Roll. My agent at the time, Valerie Kragin, had been suggesting I go and work in this Vegas show. Now, I know my limitations, and it had been a definite "no" for years. I don't sing, and I don't dance. I'm lucky if I can get across the street some days. I had told her "no" on numerous occasions.

During summer in Los Angeles, the industry dries up. That's how I ended up shooting for Playboy. This June in 1990 it was no different. Valerie was begging. Seems the Sands Hotel had a contract that the show *must* have a Playboy Playmate. The Playmate was to come out of a giant centerfold prop assisted by a group of dancers and dance with them during that number. She then would do a five- ten-minute stand-up comedy act, and then come out dancing for the Grand Finale. Not a particularly hard gig, but I had no stage experience. Doing this show meant I would relocate for six months as well.

After some research I figured that if I went, since I would be doing the show at night, I could get a modeling agency in Las Vegas, and also pick up some extra money doing conventions in the daytime as well. It actually was an excellent opportunity to make good money and put it all away. I would have zero expenses. After I signed the contract, I moved to Las Vegas.

The day I arrived I saw the show with Valerie Kragin and the director of entertainment for the Sands Hotel and Casino. I rehearsed the next day and by day three there I was, jammed up in this giant prop of a Playboy Magazine waiting for my official appearance. It was a complete and utter train wreck. I came out of my "magazine" with the help of the showgirls, and as soon as my feet hit the floor, I forgot every step. After coming close to kicking a dancer in the ass, it was decided that I needed another day of rehearsal. The troop was not happy to come in during the day. We worked into the night and most of them stayed up very late.

The house I was staying in I shared with the girls. Being the lead, I was given the master bedroom. None of this was really helping. The first few weeks were the toughest. The troop had been together for years and I was sharing their house and a dressing room with four of the lead singers. They were not in any hurry to get to know me. In fact, not many words were shared. This was something foreign to me. Though my time at the mansion had changed since I quit drinking, I was never shunned like this. Five nights a week the final curtain dropped at 11:30. I would then hustle out to hit a midnight 12-step meeting. I was working in the daytime, shooting commercials for hotels and doing print work. It was amazing how much work there was in Las Vegas. My schedule was very packed and the girls at the house couldn't figure out where I was all the time. They were especially curious where I went after the show. They didn't see me in the lounge or the restaurant and I wasn't home.

Finally, one of the girls spoke to me in a semi-snotty voice, asking where I was going at night.

I wasn't prepared to answer, and I really had nothing to gain, so I told them the truth. "I'm going to a midnight meeting. I'm almost three years sober."

Their eyes lit up, completely taken aback by what I had just told them. It seems they had been secretive because, like me, they had been trying very hard to get sober. One of the girls had almost 30 days and the other had maybe five. The one with almost 30 days was trying to take care of the one with almost five.

They were on their own and not doing well. One of them started to cry. As they explained the struggles of living in Vegas, away from family support, and how they felt isolated and alone, I shared part of my story. I described my working and struggling in the early days. Being on set at 90 days sober and feeling like an outcast. They joined me after the second show. At midnight, the three of us girls walked into the midnight meeting, full makeup, false eyelashes and all. By the sixth week we were joined by a few guys from the house band. The carpool was getting full, so we were joined by another car following us every night. The show became a very joyous place to work and I just loved and adored the girls.

Though our spirits were running high, tickets sales were down. Part of it had to do with it being 120° in the middle of summer and part of it was the show had been running so long in Vegas. The show manager had started to rearrange and pull tables from the showroom as not to let it appear to be not empty (pulling them closer and closer to the stage).

The dancers and singers at the Sands Hotel and Casino,
who I loved with every inch of my heart.

By the time 4th of July rolled around, The Sands' director of entertainment came to see the show. He was reevaluating what needed to be done to get attendance up and where to put more money. I thought it would be an excellent idea to hand sparklers to the dancers during the finale. Every night during the finale I pranced through the middle of the showgirls while they were lined up and we would walk to the front of the stage, bow, and the curtain would close. On this particular night I had picked up these sparklers while I had taken a quick trip home. Fireworks were illegal in Las Vegas. The stage manager had lit them, and I had 20 or so woven between my fingers. The showgirls were delighted and took them one at a time. We all made it to the front of the stage and, right about then, my sparklers started to shoot sparks out in the audience. Because the tables were now right up against the stage, people started diving under the tables. I heard loud laughs and screams, then the fire alarms went off, along with loud screeching sounds with white blinking lights. The curtains started to close and the last thing I saw was a man hitting a woman's head with his hand. A giant spark had hit her head and her hair was going up in flames.

With the curtain down, I hightailed it as fast as I could up two flights of stairs, grabbed my sweatpants, and threw them over my costume. Completely out of breath, I made into the employee parking lot, and, once safe in my car, I drove past the main entrance of the hotel and casino. There were people outside in the pajamas and fire trucks and tons of other people. They had evacuated the entire hotel and casino on 4th of July. I drove straight to our rented house and waited for the phone to ring. I just sat and waited for my call of termination. As the dancers came home, one by one they asked if I was packing. I told them I had not received my call.

The following night I returned to my dressing room at my call time. There was a sign with very large writing on it:

"PLAYMATES ARE NOT ALLOWED TO PLAY WITH MATCHES."

There was never another word spoken.

I continued my midnight runs with my girls, loving them and handholding them for the remainder of my trip, realizing that my purpose was to be an example of love and kindness and to show them how to have fun at work. On my last show at the Sands, the girls all attacked me with water guns while on stage, the band played my wrong songs, and I put a giant stuffed pig in the magazine when they came to fetch me, all the while teaching them never to take oneself too seriously and to always be able to laugh at yourself.

Dona Speir

Chapter Twenty-Six
My Soul Starts to Settle

The following June, 1991, I was chosen for the Playboy broadcasting team. It was a squad of a few girls traveling to radio stations to do morning radio for a week. So, I knew I couldn't dance, and I definitely couldn't act, and I was just a mediocre model, but there was one thing I could do and that was talk. Basically, that is how I got most of my jobs. By talking my way into them. On the bottom of my resume that we attached to my headshot there was a place titled "Special Skills." Mine said: "The ability to place a noun and verb in the same sentence. Oh, and I can pick up strange objects with my feet."

I arrived in Houston working for KLOL, Houston's #1 rock station. It started with four girls and quickly dwindled to two. I took the title "Dona-Do-You-Wanna" (some things just fit) and made it work. But what happened behind the scenes is what is really important. When we originally boarded the flight to Houston, our agent was with us. One of the playmates came on the flight really late, late as in the very last person and barely making it. She came staggering drunk down the aisle wearing a wrinkled dress, a crumpled hat, and carrying a bridal bouquet. It was quite the sight. She was drunk, laughingly announcing that she had caught the bouquet at a wedding. She flopped down next to me and proceeded to pass out, her head in my lap. I shared a room with that gal the entire time. Night after night she came back inebriated. It was a mirror of myself and what I did to all my other Playmate roommates. I lovingly put her to bed and when asked about how I stopped drinking, I shared. I knew one more time that the radio show didn't matter. My bigger purpose in life was to be where I was asked. Nothing more. If only to be an example of a woman with integrity.

One day after being on the air, I came back to the hotel. My roommate had gone back up to the room to sleep while I went to the pool. There was no one there. I dove into the pool and when I came up I was standing. It seemed the entire world had stopped. There was no movement whatsoever. No breeze, no sound, nothing. Just myself. I could not tell where the pool water stopped and the air started. I was completely at peace with myself and the world. I just stood there and had this incredible overwhelming feeling inside my core that no matter what happened in my life, from that moment on, if I never took another drink, I would be all right. My soul had settled. I was being set free from myself.

Chapter Twenty-Seven
Motherhood (and other absurdities)

By 1993 I was 29 years old. I wasn't sure if I was old or if I had just run my course. Either way, I couldn't get a modeling job if I tripped over it. It had been almost 15 years since I stood as a little girl in a leotard in Jack's house. I had traveled the world and seen things most people write books about (ha!). I felt more fortunate than anyone in the world. Blessed beyond belief. I had worked with Baryshnikov, been dressed by Bob Mackie, chased by screaming fans in the Tokyo airport, shot in the sands of San Tropez, been on billboards in Manhattan, dined with presidents of countries, and more. But that was all behind me.

In 1991, I met yet another husband-to-be. Completely not my type. Tall, goofy, and preppy. I wasn't overly interested in a relationship when I met him. My life was fine as it was. I was single, living alone, traveling for work with tons of girlfriends. I was truly happy with who I was and where I was going. Maybe it was my aloof attitude or my lack of interest that made him so damn persistent. At this time, I seemed to stop worrying what people thought of me. I was living a truly free life. Then I fell in love. He was to be the true love of my life. When I walked down the aisle July 11th, 1992, the love of my life and I said our "I dos." There was never a man I loved more. Except my dad, of course. I knew I would spend the rest of my life with this man. So in 1993 when we talked about having a child (which I swore my entire life I would never do) I said yes.

Within 30 days I was pregnant. I then understood why God gave me nine months to get ready for this brilliant brainstorm. In my life, I had never babysat, changed a diaper, or been around babies. In fact, during all my travels, when I went to the desk at the airlines, I always asked to be seated as far away from children as possible. I was definitely not the maternal type. It wasn't that I disliked children—I just had never been around them. During my pregnancy I belonged to a small group of women who were pregnant at the same time. They seemed to be enjoying their pregnancy a lot more than I did. I had a terrible first trimester. But, then again, in my entire life I never felt more beautiful than I did when I was pregnant. In 15 years of the world's best makeup artists and stylists, they could never have done to me what this baby did to me on the inside. For most of my life I had to be perfect. A size two. Nails always done, hair always done, legs always shaved, always ready for that next job, that next interview. Finally, I was relaxed. As the baby grew inside of me, I was slowly getting bigger and it was beautiful. I wore dresses for the first time in my life, flower prints. And I stopped wearing black. I felt like a girl at last. I know that sounds strange but being pregnant brought out my feminine side. It was lovely and I loved it. Looking down and seeing the little movements in my stomach excited me. It was a blissful feeling. My insides had finally caught up with my outsides. I was told we were having a girl. I had wanted a little girl. A beautiful little girl. We named her Emily Grace. I was so excited for her. I envisioned this cute little princess. She and I shopping, dressing alike, looking alike, being alike. I was completely delusional. What I wanted was a doll. I had no idea about babies. Then at around six months I passed a kidney stone. Alone in the emergency room I was told Emily had a penis. How could they have made such a mistake? I was devastated. There was no consoling me. Once again that thought of worthlessness came back to me, that feeling that I was defective and that, no matter what, everything in the world that I secretly wanted would never happen. I was always number two and I would always have to settle. My self-worth was always a struggle and my relationship with God was harsh. In my eyes, if you truly knew me, you knew I really wasn't worthy of a child, let alone a little girl. That God was punishing me still. I was heart sickened. My loving husband tried. He removed all the little girl clothing out of the nursery and lined the hallway into his room with adorable baby boy clothing, but it just didn't seem right. Depression seemed to fill me to my core.

On October 17, 1994, I delivered a six-pound little boy. We named him "Grayson" because we had been "graced with a son." I had had an emergency cesarean because I had become so sick, losing weight in the last weeks of my pregnancy, having the flu, a high fever, and more medical problems. I had had a difficult pregnancy starting with the first few months, but he was a fighter. The day my son was born was the best and I would eventually understand later to be the worst day of my life. The best day because I would eventually know the true meaning of life. The lessons that my son would teach me and the memories we would share as a mother and son. The worst because my husband started with a company that would slowly take him away from our family. Right at delivery my little boy was extremely sick and went into ICU, and the love of my life started his new career.

I remember the day I finally got to see my son. They had whisked him away so quickly after delivery. I was only allowed to hold him briefly. He was in an incubator with an IV in his head. He looked so little and sick. Once again I felt it was my fault, that I had done something wrong. I had internalized it. That I had harmed my baby. They never brought him to my room until close to the day I was released from the hospital. For the first time ever, I changed a diaper. *Woo-hoo*, I thought, *where are the nurses to tell me what an outstanding job I've done?* And then came the moment I was to take him home. I could not believe that anyone in their right mind would allow me to walk out of an institution with this little helpless being. Didn't they know who I was? Someone who had avoided little noisy creatures her entire life? The girl who had never cooed at a little baby before? A girl so selfish that once her girlfriends had babies I slowly moved away because I had no interest. I was stunned that they would let anyone walk out with a baby. All you had to do was have one and there you go. Put him in a little plastic car seat that I could barely figure out and I could take him away from real professionals? Were they mad? They were really going to let me take him? What had this crazy world come to?

After six days in the hospital, Grayson and I came home. I was completely clueless. I walked in the door scared to death, and this started the beginning of a harrowing postpartum depression. I had no clue about this. I wasn't even out of the hallway yet.

I looked at my husband and said, "I think we made a huge, mistake, what are we going to do?" I was completely serious.

The love of my life was in a hurry to get back to work and just shrugged it off as my twisted sense of humor. Between my complete ability to be upfront in-your-face honest and my odd humor, he just kept walking.

My husband had to go back to work. I was extremely sick with a high fever and I was grateful my sister was there. Still recovering from an emergency cesarean, this was the beginning of the change of my relationship with my husband.

Laying in the bed a few nights later, baby in the bassinet, there was a large bottle of Vicodin on my nightstand for pain from my Caesarian. My husband had gone to a concert with his work associates. I begged him not to go. The baby was ten days old and I was beginning to get well physically but not emotionally. My fever had broken yet I was lying there staring at what looked like the world's biggest bottle of Vicodin. Grayson was getting well and *I'm staring at the Vicodin*. Once an addict, always an addict. The obsession had kicked in for drugs. Once they had given them to me and they were in my system, all I wanted was more. That craving had set in. Was it two every four hours? Four every two hours? I was watching the clock, waiting for the time to pass so I could take them because I wanted them. I needed them.

I had fought for Grayson's health for nine months. He had fought to stay alive for nine months. I spent three months on bed rest because I was bleeding. It had been touch and go. I passed a kidney stone without drugs so he wouldn't be affected. I had to have an emergency cesarean because I was sick and it endangered him. Then he was in the ICU because he was so sick.

Years without a drink or drug and I still honestly was having to make a conscious decision between my baby and drugs. He was crying in his bassinet and I was thinking about taking the fucking Vicodin. I put the pillow over my stapled stomach, rolled out of the bed, and flushed the entire bottle of Vicodin. Fuck, would this ever end?

It felt like my postpartum was something that needed to be treated with an exorcism. Also, worst of all, I did not bond with Grayson. In fact, I felt the baby was destroying my marriage. I felt separated from my family and was having thoughts of harming the baby. I would get up with him at night to feed him and the thought of putting a pillow over his head was very strong. He had colic and I had not slept in days. Susan Smith was all over the news at this time for driving her children into a lake. I completely understood why she did that. I empathized with her. It made perfect sense to me.

People asked me how motherhood was and I responded, "It's the most overrated thing I've ever done," not understanding their put-off reactions. I just didn't have that maternal loving instinct. And what was worse, it didn't matter.

I had all but stopped showering and I looked tired all the time. Wasn't that the look of a new mother? My husband was hardly around because of his new job. People said it would be okay and subside. They said it was "The Baby Blues," but by two months it was just getting worse, mostly because of the colic. He was up all night and wouldn't nurse. I sat in the nursery night after night listening to this screaming infant, wondering why I had him. Everything in my life had become challenging. I wasn't eating enough calories for him to nurse or for me to pump milk. I had completely lost my appetite. I was lethargic. I wasn't thinking clearly and pulling myself together was becoming harder and harder. I was a terrible mom. People wanted to see the baby. I told my husband to put him in the window so that people could drive by and look. I had no desire for human interaction or conversation. I watched day after day as my handsome husband dressed to leave for work in the morning, leaving me behind. Days rolled on.

Taking care of the baby became harder and harder. Bathing, feeding, and dressing him. I didn't really leave the house. My husband called midmorning one day. I was in the car driving. I very rarely left the house, let alone with the baby. I was supposed to get Grayson's little hands and feet made into ceramic Christmas ornaments. I was already weeks late. It was something I had been so excited about before the delivery. All those little things you say you will do while pregnant. The baby book sat dusty, the photos I was going to take never taken, the announcement I was going to send immediately not printed or sent. He asked where I was going. I must have given him a vague answer because he knew something was very wrong in my voice.

I was on my way to a fancy neighborhood in Newport Beach. I had decided that morning to leave the baby on a doorstep. I just didn't want him anymore. He needed to go. He was the problem in my life. He was the reason my husband was away so much. He was the reason we argued so much. I had him bundled up in his car seat. It was apparent I had lost my mind and was emotionless. My husband told me to turn the car around he would be home immediately. That afternoon we were in front of a psychiatrist. The doctor asked me if I ever had any thought of harming the baby.

I answered, "Every day."

No one even blinked. Including me.

I wasn't allowed to be left alone with the baby. I didn't understand why, but that was fine with me. I had no interest in even being with him. The scary thing was I had no idea how bad I had gotten. I knew I was miserable, but I really believed my thinking was normal. That it really was in the best interest to all if I got rid of the baby. It was all his fault.

I was immediately treated for postpartum depression and I saw color for the first time in months. I remember finally sitting in the nursery holding my son in his glider at night. Looking at the wonder of him and the beauty of the silence. Well, almost—he was still screaming. But I had compassion. Love. My beautiful baby boy. My beautiful Grayson. Just him and me. He was an amazing gift from above. How I loved him so. I held him so close to my chest. It only took a few days. The beginning of the wonders of parenting. He was such a joy. So much mischief. And to think I almost missed it all.

I almost missed it all.

Chapter Twenty-Eight
Life Can Still Be Messy

Grayson grew up and so did my passion to help others. He was a happy, mischievous child. Always hiding things and dragging me around to find them. He was the light of my life. I was holding 12-step meetings at my home and working with a ton of young women. I took classes in lots of exciting interests and had a wonderful life. Unfortunately, my marriage didn't grow.

While I volunteered in different places for women, the love of my life worked and worked and worked. Though he and I were broke when we got together and our first home was just 850 square feet, we began to receive the gifts of life. We bought second and third homes. We bought yachts. We joined country clubs and traveled extensively. When I first met him, we were both living in rented apartments. He owned a ranch in Texas but owed the IRS a ton of money. It didn't matter to me. We slowly moved through the trials of life. Our first little house was in my name because of his bad credit. So bad his credit card was taken away on our honeymoon. But we were such young newlyweds it didn't matter to me. It was always my dream to start with nothing and grow a life with a partner. We moved to Irvine, into a young couple neighborhood where I planted flowers and we knew all the neighbors. It was in that little cookie-cutter home that Grayson was born and my husband's first big job took off. After two to three years of marriage, the money started to roll in. We purchased the big 6,500-square-foot home. Funny, it was never what I dreamt of, nor was it how I was raised. The neighbors were farther apart and we began to have live-in help. I spent more time helping others, volunteering in shelters for woman. The desert house on the golf course came along. The possessions began to own us. Every weekend we were away and Gray was getting older. He wanted to join soccer and be with his little friends. I wanted to be home and the pressures of work were preventing it.

Our relationship was deteriorating. Old behaviors started coming back. Rage, greed, lies, adultery, and they were destroying us. We had too much stuff and not enough faith. His work associates were charged with securities fraud and they either were on probation or went to prison. At that time, while they were in prison, he was taking care of their families as well. I felt he was paying more attention to them then to his own family. The pressure was insane. He was angry all the time, and I missed him terribly. I yearned for our simple life in our 850-square-foot condo. Or our little house in Irvine where I planted flowers and knew all the neighbors.

I tried to keep Grayson as normal as I could. Emotionally, I was still very much a child myself. We had Baskin-Robbins' cake fights together. Grayson and I would jump in the pool fully clothed every June 1st. Just to bring in summer. We collected Beanie Babies and I worked every week in Gray's school, helping out as I could, having playdates with other children and having normal couple friends. Grayson and I did everything together. While my husband golfed, Gray and I were inseparable. We would ride bicycles built for two, or play Duck, Duck, Goose. Just him and me and his stuffed animals. Him always begging me, "Pick me, Mommy, pick me!"

Chapter Twenty-Nine
Fasten My Seatbelt

I was sitting in my regular noon 12-step meeting and my cell phone would not stop blinking. Back then they were flip phones and the green light kept going off. We didn't text and I barely knew how to turn the sound off. But it was relentless. It was unusual and I knew it was either my husband or my family. I have never been the type to go outside during a meeting. I have always been taught to show up early, sit up front, and stay late. In fact, I have taken those rules into just about everything I do today. So it seemed pretty important that I went to check on the phone. I went outside to the ladies' room and saw my sister had called several times. It didn't sit right with me. Lisa and I have always been close, but not like this. My internal alarm went off. I dialed her back and received the news.

"Dona, Dad went in for some tests last week."

My heart started to pound. I knew what was coming but didn't really believe it. "What? Huh?"

"Dad, he had some things checked. Remember how you made him go to the doctor because he was losing weight? They found out today Dad has cancer. Dad has cancer."

"Lisa, no one in our family has ever had cancer, are you sure? This is a mistake. Is it lung cancer?"

"No it's not lung cancer, you need to call Mom and Dad, they will explain everything."

"Okay, okay I will."

I walked out in the sunlight.

And we hung up. I sat down on the pavement where I had been standing. Stunned. That word was foreign in our family. How could this be? Cancer? Dad? No, there must be some mistake. It was a beautiful afternoon in Newport Beach. The concrete was warm and the sun was hitting my shoulders and my back, yet nothing was moving. I slowly and reluctantly went back in the meeting and sat down. I didn't breathe a word to anyone. I was in denial. My father had been diagnosed with cancer. My daddy. The only other man I truly loved besides my husband. I had started to loose both of the men in my life at the same time. I held on to my marriage as long as I could for the sake of my child but it just wouldn't work. The rage, lies, and lust had taken over. After nine years of marriage, the love of my life and I were nearing our end, neither one of us mature enough for marriage. Our priorities were not synched. We had gotten lost along the way and we were both living lies.

On the morning of March 14, 2001, not long after that phone call, I said to him, while scrambling eggs over breakfast, "I think we should consider separating."

The very next morning, without warning, March 15, 2001, the love of my life moved out of our home. I was 14 years sober that day. My sobriety anniversary. My husband pulled our 7-year-old son over to explain to him that this was not his fault. And he left. As easy as that. Bag in hand. Boom.

I was angry. My life as I knew it came crashing down. I took my father's illness exceptionally hard. I had spent years repairing our relationship and I was devastated. I was bewildered. I was lost. Everything had happened so quickly. I had been walking on eggshells around my husband for years. He was angry and I was angry. He moved out immediately after nine and a half years and filed so he wouldn't have to pay alimony. That was the farthest thing from my mind. I was so frightened of him and his power. He would soon destroy me in the divorce. My being, my soul, and my spirit.

Chapter Thirty
Pulling Myself Up For Good

During the next few years of divorce struggles, I became a shell of a person. I myself became solely responsible for our son. Though we had mutual custody, for some reason he was never available to be a dad. I realized I was truly on my own. I had no family living near me and I was raising Grayson on my own. I was bitter, scared, and frightened. This was my biggest fear coming true. To be a single parent. Looking back now, I never wanted children because I never trusted anyone enough not to leave. I had such deep abandonment issues and here they were coming true. I was always afraid I would be a single parent and that was too much responsibility for me. I had to hire four separate attorneys to deal with my ex. I remember standing in a high-rise looking out over a parking lot with a room full of attorneys (no clue how I was going to pay them) as they were discussing my case. I was thinking two things: *one, I'm not that important, and two, I understand why people jump out of buildings.* The thought was in the front of my mind as I heard them talk in the background. I could not tell anyone for fear of my son being taken away from me. I felt complete hopelessness and apartness. Separate from the world with no way out. I was strangled in lawsuits and battles I never dreamed of. I was in over my head. I only wanted a divorce, and half of what was ours. Nothing more. My ex was an expert with the legal system. I was not. The hardest part was I was still in love with him. I was brokenhearted and my father was dying. I had never felt more alone in my life. Suicide had become an option again. Had it not been for my son, I don't think I would be here now.

And then one day it came to me. A soft whisper. *Stop fighting.* One night after I put Gray to bed it occurred to me. There was no one else in that room with me when I looked in the eyes of my husband and decided to have a baby. It was my decision. Regardless of what he did or did not do. I made the decision to have a child. It was the hardest truth about myself to swallow. I realized right then and there I could not rely on anyone but myself to provide for my son. I could not do this to myself or my son any longer. I needed to stop fighting.

No one but I alone was responsible for my decisions. I was not a victim in this world but a participant in all my actions and that's how I want my son to know me. I realized I wanted to be the best mother he could have. I wanted to give him the best education I could give him. Even though I dropped out of high school at the tenth grade. I was responsible. I'd be damned if I wasn't going to do everything I could as a single parent. Against all my attorneys' wishes and thoughts, I stopped fighting my ex-husband for all the money and signed the divorce papers. He won, but I won in the long run.

I had signed everything over to him. I just couldn't fight him anymore. I wanted my son and I wanted peace. I bought an adorable little house in an older neighborhood where Gray and his friends could run in and out the front door, and leave their bicycles with the wheels spinning on the front lawns. I knew the neighbors and we had BBQs together. The house was over 50 years old and away from all the Newport Beach nonsense. I wanted my son to be raised like I had been. At least be raised like all the good I remember. Simple and honest. With morals and manners. Everyday he had routines and chores. Not live-ins and playdates with nannies. We skateboarded outside and played in the pool with friends. The neighborhood played kick the can in the summer nights with all the adults while all the kids dressed in black.

I did everything my father had taught me. Put all my money down on a house. Paid off my cars, had no debt, and had my son. I would be able to teach him the good things in the world that came from my family. Gray and I began to have fun. Laser tag in the streets at night. Bottle rocket wars with our neighbors. Friends over all the time. For my 40th birthday, my son bought me a skateboard with pink wheels. We would skateboard together to dinner at his favorite Japanese restaurant. Millions of dollars could never replace those memories or the times I shared with my loving young man.

But I needed help financially. I was barely making ends meet. Receiving only a few hundred dollars a month in alimony wasn't helping, so I got odd jobs. I swore that if I had to scrub toilets to be home with my son I would. We didn't have much, but my bills were minimum. Thank God for Dad, for teaching me to live even when I did not have a lot. The days of the fancy vacations were gone. But the time we shared and the memories we made were priceless. I did a little convention work and a few odd modeling jobs for older women. I worked in a jewelry store part time and volunteered at a woman's recovery center. I taught PE at Gray's school and had the entire class doing the Bend and Snap. I put on large events for his school. I started my own little events company that made very little money but it allowed me to be home with him. My priority was to be home in the morning and after school and nothing was about to stop me.

Having shoulders big enough
to be a mom amongst the dads.

I started putting on events in the recovery community and was named Woman of the Year by one of the shelters. I was given awards for special acts of kindness and consideration, but in reality they were saving my son's and my life. My 12-step sponsor insisted that I do these things during the divorce. I hated her for that. She said it was important to get out of myself and to be of maximum service during these difficult

Dona Speir

times. Because I was in so much pain, I did what was suggested. The fruits of this paid off dearly.

There had been many times I had been offered to open a for-profit women's recovery home, but I just never thought it was the right time. Especially when there were so many women dying of this damned disease that had nowhere to go. I saw it every day. Even though I lived in a somewhat affluent area, I always worked hands-on in different recovery centers, shelters, and institutions. I'm no different from any of the girls I have met along the way and I have full understanding and compassion for them all. At that point two of my own gals I sponsored had already passed. I never wanted to see another young woman die again. So there I was 39 years old and about to take on the next biggest project of my life. I was about to learn true compassion and understanding to a new level.

As I was slowly coming to grips with being a single mom, I began to notice that there were women who needed a place to go to dry out and recover from alcoholism in Newport Beach. There were plenty of places that accepted insurance. There were the fancy places in Malibu and the Betty Fords of the world, but what about the women who have been kicked out by their husbands? The young gals who had been living in their cars? The ones who had been with drug dealers and beaten? The women who had been shooting dope while they were pregnant? Too afraid to tell anyone they wanted a way out? What about the daughters who needed a place to go? Or the mothers who had been wandering the streets? Where did they go? Shelters only allowed them a night or two and then kicked them back out the door, never allowing them to get on their feet. Maybe a food voucher or two. Most suffered from alcoholism or drug addiction. Where did all these beautiful creatures of God go whom no one wanted? They were here in affluent Newport Beach. Right under my nose. Filled with shame and guilt. In need of love and understanding. My circumstances might not have been so dire but my feelings were exactly the same. I always had felt like that girl, woman, mother, and daughter no one wanted with nowhere to go and no full understanding and definitely no answers. I could relate to all of it.

It was a long shot. There was one place that had a few beds but not one that was completely for free. A 501c-(3). A complete nonprofit. I had absolutely no idea how to do this but I knew people and I had a will. I was becoming stronger. I had straightened out the wreckage of my past and suddenly understood my calling in life. It's hard to pinpoint the precise moment when this revelation happened. But the feeling was clear once it formed. It was to give of myself. To love others without judgment and with full compassion. It was a feeling that came from deep inside of me. I understood that as a child at the floral shop, the concept of nurturing and helping things grow and thrive, but now it was on a new level. Now it was real and it was time to act on it.

Every week for a year and a half, a small committee met at my house. First it was two of us, then three, then four of us. An idea was born. But would it work? Could we really survive by donations and volunteers to run the house? We worked diligently with one goal in mind: *there is absolutely no reason that women should die of alcoholism any longer, just because they don't have money.* I had fought for money and it almost killed me. I was not about to allow lack of it to kill them. With seed money of $15,000 dollars, we received our nonprofit status. California Women's Recovery was born. When something is meant to be, there is no stopping the wheel. We rolled hard. Every player we needed magically appeared. A doctor on the board, an attorney on the board, a grant writer on the board. Then, incredibly, a house was presented to us. A dear friend, also an angel, had an enormous home in an unincorporated area for various reasons and rented it to us, knowing what the use would be. The $15,000 dollars given to us was from a woman who had lost her daughter from an overdose on drugs. She had been sober, received her therapist license, and relapsed. She was found in her car behind a grocery store. We dedicated our home in her honor. The Lynn House opened its doors. We had no clue how we would pay our bills or how we would keep our doors open but we had faith. We believed if we did the right thing that it would work out. We were donated a 1-800 number and had a house parent.

The day the Lynn House opened, there were girls sitting on the porch waiting to get a bed. Word had spread far. One of our first girls came from as far as Las Vegas. The phones were ringing. Unfortunately, we only had six beds. For 30 days, we fed, clothed, housed them, nurtured and loved them. We brought in speakers, drove them to 12-step meetings. We took them to doctors' appointments, to court, to the DMV, and helped with job placement. Whatever we could to help them on their feet. We partnered with other sober living environments to help facilitate resources for our girls. It was a tall order and there were plenty of bumps along the way. Learning experiences galore. I had agreed to stay as chair of the board for one year only.

At the end of my divorce and the beginning of the Lynn House, my father was extremely worried about me, being on my own in Orange County with no family and being a single parent. He knew it was terribly hard on me. Our relationship, which had truly become such a strong bond between daughter and father, had grown so much. I had nurtured it and taken care of it for years.

Though in remission for years, on a trip to Las Vegas right before the divorce, he looked ill. Worried, I rushed him into his doctors. His cancer had returned. His health had deteriorated and I had known over the last year he had been worried because of the divorce about whether I would be all right. He could no longer travel because of his illness and I wanted him to come out and see the ocean one last time. He could not fly and he could not drive himself.

I had stopped telling them about the divorce proceedings because I knew it just worried him and my mom. Concerned for my future and for Grayson, I needed to find a way to get him out of Las Vegas. Though I didn't have much money, with what I had in my savings I hired a car to drive my parents out to Newport Beach. My father needed to be able to stand up every five to ten minutes and that was the only way they could travel. I had replanted my gardens with all of his favorite flowers so he could sit in my backyard and I could do crosswords with him. He had aged tremendously in just a few months from when I had seen him. My dad. He was weaker and older than his 73 years. I drove him to the beach.

He looked at me and said weakly, "This will be the last time I see the ocean, Dona."

It devastated me. He put his hand on mine.

How could I lose him?

I drove my parents from the beach that day back to our family home in Fountain Valley and anywhere they wanted to go. I just wanted him to know when he passed that I was okay. That after all the chaos of my childhood, the divorce, me being a single parent, that his baby daughter, his daddy's girl, would be fine and he could pass in peace. Though most of this was unspoken, we both knew what this was about. When they left to return home to Las Vegas, I knew I might never see him alive again.

Only a month or two after his visit I got a call from my sister Paula. I had received numerous calls in the past, but this one was different, and I knew it. My sister Paula had moved in with my parents to help take care of my father. My mom could no longer do it by herself.

"Dona, it's bad, worse than it's ever been. Something happened today, I can't explain it," she said, bursting in tears, with terror in her voice. "Dad called out for me. It was a strange call. He was frightened. I heard it in his voice. When I got in the room, he was jerking, and then he got completely silent. He hasn't spoken since."

"What?" I burst into tears just over the sound of her frantic voice.

"Get here quickly, on the next flight, don't book a ticket, buy one at the airport," she shouted.

I went immediately to Gray's school and picked him up.

I called my ex. "This is it," I said. "I need to bring Gray to your work."

When I heard his voice on the phone my heart broke for the second time that day.

I dropped Grayson off at my ex-husbands office. I hugged my ex so tightly. I needed him. I needed something. He was the only other person who knew me well and understood how close I was to my father. I was weeping. He was already engaged to another woman.

My world was shattering around me yet again; I was losing control by the second. My feet were moving but I wasn't going anywhere. I parked at the airport and went in and bought a ticket. The woman at the counter asked if everything was all right. I couldn't answer. I just stared at her. I was completely in a daze. I knew when I returned back to this place my world would never be the same. I got on a plane and took a cab to my parents' house. Surrounding my dad's bed were my three sisters. I rushed up to the foot of his bed. I touched his foot. He looked so small, so old. Gone was the man everyone knew and talked to. The man who had a smile for everyone. That father who checked the oil in the driveway when I went to visit and washed my windshield. My daddy.

I finally spoke. "I'm here, Daddy, your favorite. It's okay now."

My sisters started laughing, knowing that we had a special bond. So very special.

I awoke that next morning, March 15, 2006, and went to a meeting knowing my father would die that day. He had not spoken a word in two days and we were told by Hospice that the time was extremely near. His organs had been shutting down and he had that terrible death rattle. I had never heard that. I had stayed up the night before swabbing his mouth with cold water because I knew he was thirsty. His hands and feet were very cold, his body protecting his vital organs to keep them working. It was my 19th sobriety birthday. I went to a noon meeting. They asked for any birthdays and I raised my hand reluctantly.

I said, "My name is Dona, I'm an alcoholic, and today I have nineteen years sober."

From the fact that no one knew me, I could tell they were skeptical, because of the amount of years sober and because I was so young. They called me to the front of the room and handed me a 19-year recovery chip while I cried. When I went home, I immediately went to my father's bedside. His breathing was labored.

"Daddy, I'm nineteen years sober today. I knew you would be proud."

Tears were rolling down my cheeks. He had walked this entire walk with me. I curled my chip in my father's hand.

As the afternoon got dark, I said my goodbye to my father, reminding him what an amazing father he was and how much I truly loved him. I thanked him for every lesson he taught me and I promised I would never let Grayson forget him. I wept. The soft music played in his room. The sun had gone down, and it was extremely cold that night in Las Vegas. My father lying quietly on the bed when he took his last breath. My 19-year chip still in his hand.

I could not watch as the coroner removed my father from his home that night. I went to another bedroom and sat by myself in shock.

When I returned to the airport, I could not find my car. I searched for over an hour in tears, not remembering where I had parked. I searched floor after floor, panic setting in, sobbing harder. I eventually found the car after wandering around for at least an hour. I had no idea what I was in store for.

Grief kicked my ass. The one person in my life that no matter what was always there. The one I turned to for advice, the one who loved me no matter what. I honestly did not think I would survive. I literally sat on the kitchen floor in my tiny house for almost 30 days crying. Leaning against the refrigerator, wondering how my sisters' lives weren't collapsing. Only pulling myself together before Grayson came home from school. The sense of loss was overbearing. I had no idea that the closest person to the one who died would be hit hardest. I didn't want the days to pass because it meant my father was farther away from me. I was entirely shattered.

Then one day a small package arrived. It was from my mother. It sat on my kitchen counter for days. I had no interest. In fact I had lost interest in just about everything. My young son asking me on the way to school if I was going to cry today. The tears streaming down my face. When I returned home from dropping him off at school I noticed the package. I opened it. Inside was my 19-year chip I had bundled up in my fathers' hand on the last morning. I just stared at it. Time froze.

Once again I heard that voice. *Stop fighting, Dona. Let go.* I know he wanted me to be happy. Just as I knew the day I brought him to the ocean and held his hand.

Dona Speir

Chapter Thirty-One
The Coin

After one year as the chair of the board for the Lynn House, I stepped aside. It was the same time as my father's death. It was time for reflection healing. To heal myself and move on. The Lynn House needed to continue to have new blood and ideas. To move forward and grow. Just as I did. The Lynn House, though changed in structure over the years, has housed almost 2,000 women to date. They have purchased their own home and continue to thrive.

I have not been involved since I stepped down as chair of the board. But, every now and then, I will be attending a meeting and hear a young girl say she got sober there, and it saved her life. I'll look in her eyes, her not knowing she saved mine. One tear at a time.

I packed and moved out of Orange County. My father's death cemented the fact that I was done there. For some reason, even though I hadn't lived in the home on Walnut Street, as long as he was alive, his spirit lived there. Once he was gone, my last tie was broken. I moved to northern California where I reside now.

I continue today as a recovery coach, juggling the lives of many young women in need. I am dedicated to healing and helping young women for the rest of my life. Though my struggles in my early life were terrible on many levels, I have come to the belief that I was made perfectly imperfect in God's eyes. I continue to grow and struggle just in smaller arenas and areas. I know that I'm only human and will never be perfect. For the first time in my life I'm comfortable in my own skin and I don't measure my insides with others' outsides anymore. I am at peace with myself. I am no longer a victim or a survivor; I am just a girl from

Fountain Valley who, like everyone else, has a story to tell. My calling is to have open arms for the next woman who can't find her way, who needs love, support, and a safe landing place. If only for a moment.

My son and I continue our marvelous adventure together. As I write this, he is a senior at Chapman University. Though we did grow up together in many ways, being a single parent is the proudest ting I have ever accomplished. I am so honored to be his mother. Our bond grows stronger every day. What I discovered about my son is he is fearless of what others think of him. He has a personal freedom of self I never had as a young person. He has taught me more than I taught him. We still do silly things together. Make videos of us singing, knock on hotel room doors and run, but, mostly, my son has always had the ability to talk freely with me without fear of my reaction. It has led to the most amazing relationship in my life.

39-year plan ✓

I recently went back to high school and got my high school diploma, not a GED, but literally sat in a classroom with high school kids who dropped out. I must add, learning algebra was as difficult as it was when I was 15. I walked in ceremony with my graduation class. All high school seniors and a few of us older folks. My son told me it was the proudest moment he ever had of me. I knew my dad was there the entire time.

And that recovery chip that I gave my dad in his last hours, it sits in my "God box" on my desk. The small decoupage box was made for me by a young woman that I helped coach through recovery. It contains everything that one "turns over to God." I often hold that chip in my hand and think not so much about what could have been, but rather what will be.

Afterword

The story between Bill Cosby and me shaped the person I am today. I spent years in therapy and have done extensive work around this topic and still wasn't quite sure how to write about it. Then the news broke. Bill Cosby was being charged in a 12-year-old sexual assault case. I had not even told my family about the relationship (or however you care to classify it). In fact, I had not spoken of it in many, many years. When the news broke, a few people who did know of the encounter called and asked if I was coming forward. People I had not talked to in years. I panicked.

My reasons for not coming forward then were many. First and foremost, my son knew nothing about it and didn't need to be dragged through any public scrutiny. Second, I personally know how vindictive Bill is. He eventually turned on me personally. I knew he would fight everything and everyone to the bloody end. I was not interested in getting sued for telling my truth. Third is, what was I going to sue him for? Money? No, all the money in the world cannot bring back the years of damage done to me. Only I have the power to take control of my well-being. I choose not to be victimized again. And lastly my experience was different from the rest. I am not sure to this day if Bill ever drugged me. Bill only pulled drugs out in front of me on one occasion. I did not take them and that is not my story to tell. I did however bring Bill hash to his home in Los Angeles. And fourth, it took me years to separate what was a "friendship" and what was predatory behavior. It wasn't until I was in my 30s that I unpacked my sexual abuse with any of these predators. I still lied for them and denied their wrongdoing.

When Bill was sentenced, I was interviewed for an article. It was the first time any of my immediate family found out. I sent them all a link. Had my parents been alive, I never would have come forward. As I continued to write my memoir, I realized that telling all of my truth, not just my selection of truth, might help other victims of abuse. My story is complex, just like my relationship with Bill. What I know today is, he knew better, he just didn't care.

Afterword by co-writer Chris Epting

When Dona Speir first reached out to me a couple of years ago to discuss my possible assistance in helping her to write her memoir, I wasn't quite sure what to think. She told me she had been a Playboy centerfold and that she had also led a fairly wild life. While interesting and certainly compelling to listen to her, I wasn't quite sure what the book was. Then she began describing her relationship with Bill Cosby and that certainly seemed like part of a theme in her life: being taken advantage of by selfish, reckless, predatory men. But then she told me about her recovery from addiction. All of a sudden, her story glowed with a much richer arc about a woman who, in the process of discovering sobriety, also discovered herself: the fighter, the survivor, the street-smart force of nature.

Everybody commits sins, everybody is addicted to something, be it alcohol or drugs or certain destructive behaviors, but those things don't have to destroy your life. If you believe in yourself and you accept yourself for who you are, you can overcome the deepest challenges. That's what I get from her story and that's why it's been such a pleasure to work with Dona.

I am proud to call her my friend and I'm anxious to see where her journey takes her, especially once her story becomes public.

Dona Speir

Acknowledgments

First I would like to express my deepest gratitude to my husband, Kim Niederman, who not only tolerated me through this process but also supported me. I love you.

I thank my immediate family Julie, Paula, Lisa, Jonathon, Grayson, and Kristi DuRose, my best friend in the world.

I also wish to thank all of the beautiful woman in my life who have helped shape me into the woman I am today: Kris Kane, Joan Major, June Nichols, Vicki Bauer, Katherine Koones, Joey Crabtree, Robin McIndoo, Mary Sheehan, Jill Dominguez, The "Dontourage," The "MFG's," and The "Wack Pack."

To Robert Scarborough, Stephen Margarella, and Harold Bauer for all of the love and moral support.

For helping me navigate the process and develop my personal brand I am grateful to Marcy Massura, Scott Mosko, Robyn Plaster, Mira Singer, Bryan Larkin, Joni Truilo-Codd, Doug Harris, Ally Irons Morris, and Spencer Stuard.

I appreciate my publisher Nell Minow at Miniver Press who took a chance on me.

I wish to thank my co-writer Chris Epting. Without him this book would never have been written. He was my therapist, my babysitter, my coach, my parent, and my best friend. He proverbially held my hand and wiped my tears, never yelled back, always encouraged me to move forward, step out my comfort zone, and, mostly, breathe.

Also, in loving memory of my mom, dad, and brother.

Dona Speir

Finally, thank you to my loving God, who I always turn to. He has never failed me and always guided my path. I am humbled and sincerely grateful.

Resources

Alcoholics Anonymous
aa.org
212-870-3400

Narcotics anonymous
Na.org
818-773-9999

Marijuana Anonymous
Marijuana-anonymous.org
800.766.6779

Cocaine Anonymous
Ca.org
310-559-2554

Crystal Meth Anonymous
Crystalmeth.org
855-METH-FREE

Gamblers Anonymous
Gamblersanonymous.org
1-800-GAMBLER

Workaholics Anonymous
Workaholics-anonymous.org
510-273-9253

Dona Speir

Sex and Love Addicts Anonymous
Slaafws.org
210-828-7900

Over Eaters Anonymous
Oa.org
505-891-2664

Al-anon
Al-anon.org
757-563-1600

Co-Dependents Anonymous (CODA)
Codependents.org
602-277-7991

Tips For Parents

I believe that most if not all of my problems were predicated by both the mental and physical abuse I suffered at the hands of "Jack" the photographer and Bill Cosby. Adults that prey on children rarely if ever consider the permanent damages they are causing to their victims. In literally one moment, a life can be destructively altered.

The organization "BARK" was founded by a parent and a digital media expert who wanted to provide an option to help protect children online without compromising their privacy. BARK empowers parents to work with their children to keep them safe. I support their efforts 100% and I am thankful that they have allowed me to share these tip sheets for helping to keep children safe from adult predators:

"Grooming is the process by which someone befriends and gains the trust of a child (and sometimes the child's friends and family) in order to take advantage of the child for sexual purposes.

To accomplish this, predators are masters at manipulation, often appearing kind and helpful. However, there are grooming signs you should be aware of, including the six stages of grooming. These red flags could mean a child is experiencing grooming by an online sexual predator.

1. Friendship Forming Stage: Targeting and Gaining Trust

The friendship forming stage is composed of conversations in which the predator tries to get introduced to the child. Predators target vulnerable children—those who are needy, unhappy, unable to talk about abuse, or have less parental oversight. Next, the predator will gather information about the child and the child's family to gain the child's trust over time. It's extremely important to be aware of new people in your life and the amount of time they spend with your child and your family. Make sure your child knows that they can talk to you about anything and that you're there to listen.

Example: Predator exchanges information with the child or parent to get personal contact information, such as email addresses or usernames for social media sites. Additionally, the predator inquires about the relationships in the household.

2. Relationship Forming Stage: Filling the Child's (or Family's) Needs

After gaining access to the child, the predator starts forming a relationship by talking to them about family and school life. Next, the predator fills some sort of need that the child or the family has to ingrain himself into their lives. This may be monetary in nature; for example, a single mother struggling to pay the bills may receive cash or offers to take care of bills.

Predators may also fill a child's desire for attention by buying them gifts, taking them places, etc. Be aware of any gifts your child may receive from other adults, especially electronic devices. Be extra cautious if someone you haven't known long offers to help in an overly generous manner.

Example: The predator tries to know more about the interest and hobbies of the child so that they can exploit them. They deceive the child into believing they are in a relationship. At this stage the predator gives soft compliments, calling them "sweetie," "cutie," etc.

3. Risk Assessment Stage: Gauging the Level of Threat

The predator at this stage tries to gauge the level of threat and danger the caregivers pose. They ask questions to see how closely the child is monitored online and in real life. They try to gauge how close the child is to the family and whether their actions will be reported and believed.

In an interview with two child sex offenders, WBIR 10NEWs reported that one of the top deterrents for predators were adults who monitor the electronic communications of the child. Close relationships, close monitoring, and a child who has been warned about predators are huge threats to a predator.

Example: Predators will ask questions like, "Are your parents around?" and "Who else uses the computer?" or "Can you delete your chats?" and "Do your parents monitor your online accounts?"

4.   Exclusivity Stage: Isolating the Child from Others

At this stage, the predator tries to gain the trust of the child completely. The predator asserts that they share a special bond. Often the concept of love and care are introduced.

A predator will look for opportunities to spend time alone with the child. They will often use sly tactics to create these situations and use this time to further reinforce the idea of a special relationship. Trips to amusement parks, offers to tutor your child for free, and other similar situations may signify that your child is being groomed. Trust your instincts should you feel something is amiss.

Examples: feelings of love and exclusiveness are expressed by the predator. Strong compliments are given. They will say things like, "You are a sweetheart," or "You are so cute when you look like that," or "I feel a deep connection with you I don't feel with anyone else."

5.   Sexual Stage: Desensitizing the Child

During the sexual stage, predators ask questions about the child's sexuality. They will ask things like, "Are you a virgin?" or will talk about masturbation. Some pedophiles talk in great depth about sexual activities with the child to desensitize them to the language and content. They do this to prepare the child for actual physical interaction.

Predators have been known to show children pictures of other children without their clothing in order to make it appear "normal" and "natural." Some even take the child swimming naked together in an effort to play to the child's natural curiosity. The predator may introduce porn videos. For this reason, it is important to maintain an open line of communication with your children and act on anything that doesn't seem typical age-appropriate sexual curiosity.

Examples: The predator gives sexual-oriented compliments, exchanges sexualized pictures, and gives body and figure descriptions. They will say things like, "you are sexy," ask the child to be their boyfriend or girlfriend, or ask for nudes and sexual text messages.

6. Conclusion Stage: Controlling the Child and Situation

The conclusion stage occurs when the pedophile begins the physical abuse. Once it begins, they will go to great lengths to maintain control. In most cases, the offender uses secrecy, blame, and even threats to keep the child from saying anything.

The predator's goal is to maintain the child's participation, all while hiding it from everyone else. If your child appears withdrawn and sullen, or if they appear fearful and depressed when it's time to see a particular person, this may be a sign that they've been conditioned to remain silent about activities with this person. Let your children know they can come to you when anyone asks them to do something they are not comfortable with — even if that person is an adult.

Examples: A predator will ask questions in this stage like, "Are you able to meet up with me alone or do your parents always have to know everything?" or "Can you sneak out of your house and meet up at a McDonald's for a treat" or "When we meet I can't wait to hug you and kiss you" or "Can you walk to our meeting place or is there a place away from your house I can pick you up in my car?" Questions like this ensure the child comes alone and the predator controls how they meet.

Part II
Grooming Signs of an Online Sexual Predator
There are a number of signs to be aware of that may suggest online grooming is taking place. Although some may seem like typical teen behavior, it's still important to watch out for:

- Wanting or asking to spend more time on the internet
- Being secretive about the sites they visit or who they are talking to online
- Switching screens when you come near them when they are on their computer or phone
- Possessing new items you haven't given them, especially electronic devices
- Using sexual language you wouldn't expect them to know or that is not age-appropriate
- Emotions that become more volatile

An informative study by the Indraprastha Institute of Information Technology found that a predator does not necessarily move sequentially through the stages. They also discovered that the relationship forming stage is the most dominant online grooming stage. In other words, more than one stage can be in process and predators do not necessarily go in any particular order.

The truth is, grooming signs can be difficult to spot. This is because sexual predators tend to also befriend parents and caregivers. Maintaining an open line of communication with your child and paying extra attention to the amount of time they spend with other adults, as well as monitoring their online activity with Bark, can help protect your child from online sexual predators.

Recognizing the signs of online grooming

Online grooming occurs when a predator initiates and cultivates a relationship with a child over the internet, culminating in sexual abuse that can include:

- Taking sexual photos
- Sending sexual messages
- Sextortion
- Meeting in real life for sexual activities
- Trafficking

The process of grooming is a purposefully slow one, as predators methodically take steps to ingratiate themselves to children and gain trust. Predators are masters at manipulation and can appear kind and helpful to mask their ulterior motives, taking advantage of a child's naïveté.

The steps below follow a general pattern of behavior consistent with online grooming. However, every situation is unique, so variations are always possible. The most important thing is to always be aware of any adult who begins taking an interest in your child.

Targeting

Predators often target vulnerable children, such as those who are emotionally vulnerable or have less parental oversight. The first interactions are pleasant and include light conversations to lure them in, making the child feel important. Many predators initiate conversations on public chat apps or in the chat section of kid's games, pretending to be younger.

Engaging
Many times, the predator tries to fill some sort of need that the child has—many times, it's an emotional need, like a child's desire for attention. They meet it by paying them compliments, listening to them, or buying them gifts. Be aware of any presents your child may receive from other adults, especially electronic devices—these may be used exclusively for communication with the predator.

Boundary testing
At this point, as the predator is deepening the relationship, he'll gauge the level of threat he's facing from the parents. He'll ask questions to see how closely the child's devices are monitored, and try to determine whether the child will be believed if the truth comes out. During this time, kids may become more secretive about their activity.

Isolating
Here, the predator meets up with the child for the first time in real life. He will try to gain the trust of the child completely, convincing them that they share a special bond.

A predator will look for opportunities to spend time alone with the child. They will often use sly tactics to create these situations and use this time to further reinforce the idea of a special relationship. Trust your instincts when something isn't right when it comes to how your child is acting.

Sexualizing
This stage culminates in sexual activity. Predators will begin to discuss sex explicitly, mentioning sexual activities with the child to desensitize them. Some predators have been known to show children pictures of other children without their clothing in order to make it appear more normal. They'll also introduce sexual information that typical children of their age group would not be familiar with.

Controlling
When a predator starts to abuse a child, they will go to great lengths to maintain control and ensure that the child is dependent on them. In

most cases, the offender uses secrecy, blame, and even threats to keep children from saying anything.

Let your children know they can come to you when anyone asks them to do something they are not comfortable with, even if that person is an adult.

What you can do

Children of any gender, any family situation, and any socioeconomic level may be targeted as victims of grooming—no one is immune. To help protect your child from online predators, there are a number of steps you can take, including:

- Encourage your child to be share aware by talking openly and often about what sites they're visiting, games they're playing, and people they're chatting with.
- Create a family environment where your child feels safe talking about difficult topics. The safer a child feels, the more likely they are to open up when something bad happens.
- Monitor their devices for potentially harmful communications. Bark is specially designed to capture messaging that may be inappropriate or indicative of sexual abuse.

The truth is, grooming signs can be difficult to spot. This is because sexual predators tend to also befriend parents and caregivers. Maintaining an open line of communication with your child and paying extra attention to the amount of time they spend with other adults, as well as monitoring their online activity with Bark, can help protect your child from online sexual predators.

For more information about BARK, visit TK

The signs of drug and alcohol addictions very from person to person. As you read my memoir the first half of my abuse was almost directly related to drug abuse. The second from alcohol. Both addictions have similar warning signs. Behavioral, Social and Physical. I will try to cover the warning signs of both, but please be aware that they are not all or one. As each addict is different, so are there signs. I cannot stress enough that this is a deadly disease killing more men and woman than_____, and should always be taken seriously and with caution. If you or a loved one is suffering any of the item I state below I suggest you seek medical treatment immediacy.

Social signs of drug or alcohol use:
- Withdrawing from normal family functions and or isolating. Using or drinking alone
- Having to have a few drinks before going out to a social function.
- Having legal issues
- Giving up things that previously made you happy. Hobbies, friends, social actives after school or work.
- A socially awkward person may become more "outspoken" or an outspoken person becomes shy
- Your social reputation is dropping because of bad behavior while using or drinking
- You are seeking lower companionship to justify "I'm really not as bad as they are"
- Destroys relationships- by lying about how much drinking or using. And your Whereabouts.
- Unaccounted for time
- Financial problems—steal or borrow money, owing money
- Secrecy
- Take risks for drugs and alcohol- trading their body for drugs or alcohol, dealing drugs for money, driving drunk with kids in the car.
- Continues drinking or using even though it is causing trouble with your family/friends

Physical signs of drug or alcohol use:
- Weight, loss or gain depending upon which dependency
- Severe mood swings- crying, screaming, overjoyed,
- Slurred speech, red eyes, track marks, runny nose, nodding out, itchy nose, Nose bleeds, dilated pupils
- Hyper activity/ inability to sleep/ awake for days
- Change in eating, sleeping patterns
- Change in health care- brushing teeth, washing clothes, showering
- Paranoia

- Passing out or blacking out
- No memory of and incidences
- Getting sick or getting over being sick because of drinking or drug usage
- Having to drink or use more than you once did to get the physical effects
- Continues drinking or using even though is causing depression, anxiety, memory loss or health problems.

Behavioral signs of dependency

- Making excuses
- Defensive about their intake of drugs or alcohol- it their right, their body, if you had my problems you'd drink/use too.
- Denial—It's not really that bad. I won't die. I'm not an addict/alcoholic, addicts and alcoholics are_____ (whatever their mind see that they are, usually not them) I only drink/use this much or a this time of day.
- Beginning to show up at Dr's or hospitals for drug or alcohol consumption
- Losing jobs and families due to consumptions
- Medication shopping at different Doctors and clinics for multiple prescriptions-
- Lack of ambition, efficiency
- Inability to stop drugs or alcohol on their own or stay stopped. Drinking or doing more than intended—I'll have just one.

Made in the USA
San Bernardino, CA
28 July 2020

76095041R00122